LENAE BULTHUIS

My Prayer Diary

It's Me, Jesus

CRC Publications, GEMS Girls' Clubs

Copublished by CRC Publications, 2850 Kalamazoo Ave. SE, Grand Rapids, MI 49560 and GEMS Girls' Clubs, 1333 Alger SE, Grand Rapids, MI 49510.

We welcome your comments. Call 1-800-333-8300 or e-mail us at editors@crcpublications.org.

Library of Congress Cataloging-in-Publication Data

Bulthuis, Lenae, 1968-
It's me, Jesus : my prayer diary /
Lenae Bulthuis.
p. cm.
Summary: A devotional prayer journal with daily scripture readings and activities for each day of twelve weeks.
ISBN 1-56212-504-4
1. Girl—Prayer books and devotions—English. 2. Christian life—Juvenile literature. 3. Devotional calendars—Juvenile literature. [1. Prayer books and devotions. 2. Devotional calendars. 3. Christian life.] I. Title.
BV4860.B86 1999
242'.62--dc21 99-047616

10 9 8 7 6 5 4 3 2 1

To my husband, Michael, and our three daughters, Elizabeth, Stephanie, and Melanie. I am so blessed that God has given you to me! I love you.

To my soul mate, Diane. Thank you again for your invaluable critiques and your listening, understanding ear.

Above all, thanks and glory and praise be to God. His strength is perfect.

Contents

Preface

Jesus has been my friend and Savior since I was a small girl. I learned about him from my dad and mom, my church, and the Christian school I attended.

As I was growing up, one of the things that I learned is that Jesus wants me to read my Bible and pray to him every day. I love to read, so most of my personal devotion time was spent in studying my Bible.

Since I felt that my "real" time with Jesus was during my Bible reading, I didn't spend too much time in prayer. To me, prayer was just a nice way to begin my devotional time or a good thing to do before I fell asleep at night. And of course, I used prayer for emergency situations. I sent lots of 911 calls to heaven—prayers like "Please help my grandpa who is sick" or "Please don't let my math teacher assign so much homework!"

I didn't discover the life-changing power and importance of prayer until I was twenty-six years old. When I began writing down my prayers in a journal, I started to experience the intimacy and peace that comes from having one-on-one conversations with God. He hears! He answers! He cares!

In my journal I focus on the four parts of prayer—praise, confession, asking, and thanksgiving. I date the request and then date God's answer. My prayer time has become the best time of the day.

God wants your prayer time be the best part of your day too! Maybe, like me, you already know that personal devotions are important. But knowing it's important and experiencing an intimate friendship with Jesus are two different things. *It's Me, Jesus* can change your prayer life. If you don't know Jesus and his love for you, this book will introduce you to him. You'll discover that he's longing to be your Savior and best friend.

My prayer for you is that *It's Me, Jesus* will help build your relationship with Jesus through Bible study *and prayer!* Don't wait another day to start your prayer adventure. Jesus is waiting to hear from you today!

W E E K 1 O N E   S U N D A Y ________ (DATE)

Theme for the Week: Responsibility

Key Verse for the Week

Don't let anyone look down on you because you are young, but set an example for the believers in speech, in life, in love, in faith and in purity.

—1 Timothy 4:12

Bible Reading: 1 Timothy 4:12

Responsible in Speech

When's the last time you lost a homework assignment or forgot to feed your pets? Not too long ago, if you're like many of us! When that happened, did somebody ask, "When will you learn to be more responsible?"

You're never too young to be responsible—it says so in our verse for the week. "Don't let anyone look down on you because you are young, but set an example for the believers in speech, in life, in love, in faith and in purity." You can keep growing in responsibility, just as you keep growing older and taller.

People trust you when you're responsible in what you say. They know that you'll follow through with your promises. Think about it. While you're eating breakfast, it's easy to promise your mom that you'll wash the dishes right after school. The hard part begins when you come home that afternoon. What will happen? Will you start washing the dishes immediately, or will someone have to remind you three times?

You can please your parents, teachers, and, most importantly, Jesus, by being responsible in your speech. Tell the truth, and do what you promised!

Something to Think About

Make it your lifetime goal to be responsible in speech, life, love, faith, and purity. Ask Jesus to help you begin today!

Dear Jesus,

I praise you for ______________________

____

____

I'm sorry for ______________________

____

____

I ask you for ______________________

____

____

I thank you for ______________________

____

______________________ Amen.

Honey-Sweet Finger Sandwiches

Is your speech sweet as honey—and responsible too? Treat your tongue with these sweet sandwiches!

What You Need

White or wheat bread
1 banana, sliced
1 tablespoon peanut butter
1 teaspoon honey
Dash of cinnamon

How to Do It

1. Ask an adult for permission to work in the kitchen.
2. Toast two pieces of bread, then cut off crusts.
3. Spread peanut butter on one slice of bread.
4. Place banana slices on top of peanut butter.
5. Drizzle honey over bananas.
6. Sprinkle with cinnamon.
7. Top with remaining slice of bread, cut sandwich into four squares, and enjoy!

WEEK 1 ONE — MONDAY ______ (DATE)

Theme for the Week: Responsibility

Key Verse for the Week

Don't let anyone look down on you because you are young, but set an example for the believers in speech, in life, in love, in faith and in purity.

—1 Timothy 4:12

Bible Reading: 1 Thessalonians 4:11-12

Responsible in Life

My grandfather was a quiet, hardworking man. He didn't speak in front of church or large groups. He didn't win any fancy awards. He wasn't famous for anything.

When Grandpa died, there were no letters from the president or telephone calls from the governor. Instead, people who knew and loved Grandpa talked about how he loved Jesus with all his heart. They remembered how he cared for his family, showed kindness to his neighbors, and was responsible in all that he did.

At his funeral the pastor read today's Bible verses, 1 Thessalonians 4:11-12: "Make it your ambition to lead a quiet life, to mind your own business and to work with your hands, just as we told you, so that your daily life may win the respect of outsiders and so that you will not be dependent on anybody."

Are you responsible in your daily life? Do your parents and friends notice how you live quietly, mind your own business, and work without complaining? Do people know you love Jesus by the way you live?

Something to Think About

Jesus isn't overly concerned about how many awards you've earned, how many instruments you know how to play, or how popular you are. What's important to Jesus is how much your love for him shows in your everyday life.

Dear Jesus,

I praise you for ______________________________

____

____

I'm sorry for ______________________________

____

____

I ask you for ______________________________

____

____

I thank you for ______________________________

____

______________________________ Amen.

Family Job Jar

What You Need

A glass jar

Small pieces of paper

How to Do It

1. Invite your family for a family meeting to explain the job jar idea.
2. Ask them to think of jobs or projects that need to be done around the house and yard.
3. Write one job on each piece of paper.
4. Put the slips of paper in the jar.
5. On Saturdays (or after school), have someone draw a job from the jar.
6. Work together as a family (responsibly!) on the project.
7. When you're finished, celebrate together!

Theme for the Week: Responsibility

Key Verse for the Week

Don't let anyone look down on you because you are young, but set an example for the believers in speech, in life, in love, in faith and in purity.

—1 Timothy 4:12

Bible Reading: Matthew 5:43-48

Responsible in Love

Do you love your best friend?

____ yes ____ no

Do you love your favorite teacher?

____ yes ____ no

I'm sure you answered yes to both of those questions! But guess what? According to the Bible, there's nothing too special about loving your best friend and your favorite teacher. Even people who aren't Christians love the people who love them back.

Jesus says, "If you love those who love you, what reward will you get? Are not even the tax collectors doing that?" (Matthew 5:46). He also says, "I tell you: Love your enemies and pray for those who persecute you, that you may be sons of your Father in heaven" (Matthew 5:44-45).

You may not feel like loving your enemies. In fact, you may never feel like loving the boy who teases you at recess or the girl who always talks about you behind your back. The kind of responsible love Jesus is talking about isn't something you *feel,* it's something you *do* because Jesus loved you first.

Something to Think About

Having trouble loving your enemies? Start praying for them. God may amaze you by changing their hearts—and yours too!

Dear Jesus,

I praise you for ______________________________

____

____

I'm sorry for ______________________________

____

____

I ask you for ______________________________

____

____

I thank you for ______________________________

____

______________________________ Amen.

Breadstick Hearts

What You Need

1 (11 ounce) package of refrigerated breadstick dough

2 tablespoons (30 mL) butter, melted

Optional toppings: garlic salt, cinnamon sugar, sesame seeds

How to Do It

1. Ask an adult for permission to work in the kitchen.
2. Heat the oven to 350°. Lightly grease a baking sheet.
3. Unroll and separate dough into 8 strips.
4. Place dough on cookie sheet and shape each strip into a heart.
5. Brush dough with melted butter and sprinkle with optional toppings.
6. Bake for 15 minutes or until golden brown.
7. Serve warm. While you're eating, tell your family what you learned today about being responsible in love.

Theme for the Week: Responsibility

Key Verse for the Week

Don't let anyone look down on you because you are young, but set an example for the believers in speech, in life, in love, in faith and in purity.

—1 Timothy 4:12

Bible Reading: Ephesians 6:14-17

Responsible in Faith

Faith. Jesus wants your faith in him to grow stronger every day. He wants you to believe with your whole heart that he loves you—so much that he died and rose again to save you from your sins. Jesus wants you to trust him always to provide and care for you.

Faith. Satan fights your faith every day. He hopes that you will doubt Jesus' love for you. It would give Satan great pleasure if you quit believing in Jesus.

If you've ever had a grandma or someone you love who was dying of cancer or some other terrible disease, you know that it's tough to believe that Jesus is taking care of her. And if your mom or dad ever lost her or his job, you realize how hard it can be to believe that Jesus is going to take care of all your needs. Whenever it becomes difficult to believe in Jesus' love and care for you, Satan's arrows are attacking you.

The Bible tells you how to protect yourself from Satan's attacks. "In addition to all this, take up the shield of faith, with which you can extinguish all the flaming arrows of the evil one" (Ephesians 6:16).

Something to Think About

Protect yourself from Satan's attacks and arrows with your shield of faith! Always remember that Jesus loves you and cares for you.

Dear Jesus,

I praise you for ______________________________

____

____

I'm sorry for ______________________________

____

____

I ask you for ______________________________

____

____

I thank you for ______________________________

____

______________________________ Amen.

Armor of God Word Find

Ephesians 6:10-17 lists the armor of God that Christians need to wear in order to fight off Satan. Find the following armor piece words.

BELT	RIGHTEOUSNESS
BREASTPLATE	SALVATION
FAITH	SHIELD
FEET	SPIRIT
HELMET	SWORD
READINESS	TRUTH

Y	H	E	A	D	L	C	V	P	O	K	Y	D	B	L	X	A
G	K	T	R	B	L	X	O	D	X	B	R	E	Q	Z	L	W
T	H	X	I	I	P	H	S	S	R	O	L	S	D	N	N	M
B	H	C	T	A	G	M	P	E	W	T	N	U	M	C	I	C
E	C	R	I	S	F	H	A	S	J	F	U	H	K	L	J	U
T	E	Y	O	V	K	S	T	S	M	R	K	F	J	K	O	P
F	C	Y	E	Y	T	H	S	E	H	V	C	U	Z	D	F	X
U	T	A	T	P	E	P	B	K	O	I	E	O	W	B	L	I
L	M	J	L	L	I	L	D	S	T	U	E	B	D	K	Q	D
I	N	A	M	R	E	M	X	B	J	J	S	L	K	F	F	P
Q	T	E	I	B	U	R	Y	K	N	U	S	N	D	I	C	G
E	T	T	S	V	G	R	A	N	C	I	U	H	E	L	L	E
G	R	M	B	S	C	J	I	N	O	I	I	Q	T	S	O	L
V	P	C	K	M	N	B	A	U	D	K	Q	Z	M	U	S	Q
P	Q	W	R	V	A	I	F	P	O	S	T	E	E	F	R	X
V	D	Q	Q	N	V	X	N	O	I	T	A	V	L	A	S	T
R	E	A	D	I	N	E	S	S	P	H	J	V	B	J	R	F

Theme for the Week: Responsibility

Key Verse for the Week

Don't let anyone look down on you because you are young, but set an example for the believers in speech, in life, in love, in faith and in purity.

—1 Timothy 4:12

Bible Reading: Philippians 4:8-9

Responsible in Purity

Have you ever been shopping and had trouble deciding which T-shirt to buy? Hmmm . . . the navy or white one? That's when your mom might be tempted to take over: "Get the navy one. I'll never be able to keep the white one white!"

You know how it goes. White shirts are always bright in the mall. A couple of grass stains, spilled ice-cream sundaes, and countless washings later, those snowy T-shirts have faded to a dull cream color.

Like a bright white, brand-new shirt, Jesus wants your thoughts, words, and actions to be pure. "Finally . . . whatever is true, whatever is noble, whatever is right, whatever is pure, whatever is lovely, whatever is admirable—if anything is excellent or praiseworthy—think about such things" (Philippians 4:8).

Being responsible in purity means choosing wisely—from the books you read and the TV shows you watch to the way you treat your little brother. Let everything you think, everything you say, and everything you do be pleasing and praiseworthy to God.

Something to Think About

Does your heart look dull or dirty from sin? Here's good news! Ask Jesus to forgive you, and he'll make it whiter than snow! (Psalm 51:7).

Dear Jesus,

I praise you for ______________________________

____

____

I'm sorry for ______________________________

____

____

I ask you for ______________________________

____

____

I thank you for ______________________________

____

______________________________ Amen.

Purity Poster

It's easy to find TV commercials, magazine advertisements, and even posters that aren't pleasing and praiseworthy to God. So maybe you'd like to create your own poster for your room—one that's filled with good things!

What You Need

Posterboard
Magazine pictures that you can cut out
Glue
Scissors
Marker (optional)

How to Do It

1. Cut out pictures of people, flowers, sunsets, animals, and so on.
2. Glue the pictures on the posterboard in a collage.
3. Add a caption with the marker if you like—something like "Think About These Things . . . "
3. Hang the poster in your bedroom. Let it be your testimony!

FRIDAY ________ (DATE)

Theme for the Week: Responsibility

Key Verse for the Week

Don't let anyone look down on you because you are young, but set an example for the believers in speech, in life, in love, in faith and in purity.

—1 Timothy 4:12

Bible Reading: Colossians 3:23-24

Responsible in Work

Making your bed, hanging up your coat, and bringing out the garbage may not be on your top ten list of favorite things to do each day. But they're probably on your responsibility list!

Being responsible requires effort. You've found out by now that it takes work to be responsible in your work! The Bible tells us: "Whatever you do, work at it with all your heart, as working for the Lord, not for men" (Colossians 3:23).

So when your mom or dad asks you to rake the leaves or bring in the groceries, do it cheerfully, and do your best. It's your responsibility. You're not just doing it for your parents, you're working for the Lord!

Did you know that responsibility also has its rewards? Just read the next verse: " . . . since you know that you will receive an inheritance from the Lord as a reward. It is the Lord Christ you are serving" (Colossians 3:24). As Christians, our inheritance is eternity in heaven. Allowances or paychecks can't compare to the glory of living with Jesus!

Something to Think About

The next time you're asked to do some chore you're not real excited about, pray while you're working. Ask Jesus to help you do your best. Remember that you're serving and glorifying him by being responsible in your work.

Dear Jesus,

I praise you for ____________________

____

____

I'm sorry for ____________________

____

____

I ask you for ____________________

____

____

I thank you for ____________________

____

____________________ Amen.

Occupation Word Scramble

Read the clues and unscramble the words.

1. This person is responsible for putting out fires.

   ___ ___ ___ ___ ___ ___ ___ ___ ___ ___ ___ (GREHIFRITFE)

2. This person is responsible for helping you get well when you're sick.

   ___ ___ ___ ___ ___ ___ (TRODCO)

3. This person is responsible for helping you learn.

   ___ ___ ___ ___ ___ ___ ___ (RATCEEH)

4. This person is responsible for helping passengers travel long distances in a short time.

   ___ ___ ___ ___ ___ (ILPTO)

W E E K 1 O N E S A T U R D A Y ________
(DATE)

Theme for the Week: Responsibility

Key Verse for the Week

Write the key verse for the week on the lines below.

____

____

____

____

—1 Timothy 4:12

This Week I Learned . . .

Sunday
People will trust what I say if I'm responsible in my speech. I need to tell the truth and keep my promises. (1 Timothy 4:12)

Monday
A life of responsibility may not bring me fame or special awards. But it will earn the respect of my parents and teachers, and, most important, it will please and honor Jesus. (1 Thessalonians 4:11-12)

Tuesday
Being responsible in love goes beyond loving those who are easy to love. It means loving my enemies too. (Matthew 5:43-48)

Wednesday
Jesus wants my faith in him to grow stronger each day. I can fight off Satan's attacks with my shield of faith. (Ephesians 6:14-17)

Thursday
To be responsible in purity, my thoughts, words, and actions must be pleasing and praiseworthy to God. (Philippians 4:8-9)

Friday
While I'm working, I need to remember that I'm serving the Lord. Being responsible in work has eternal rewards! (Colossians 3:23-24)

Something to Think About

Are you growing in responsibility? In what ways?

____

____

____

Dear Jesus,

I praise you for ______________________________

____

____

I'm sorry for ______________________________

____

____

I ask you for ______________________________

____

____

I thank you for ______________________________

____

______________________________ Amen.

Favorite Cheese and Crackers

What You Need

½ stick butter
8-ounce package cream cheese
2 jars Old English cheese
Snack crackers

How to Do It

1. Ask an adult for permission to work in the kitchen.
2. Use a mixer to whip the butter, cream cheese, and Old English cheese.
3. Serve the cheese and crackers to your family, and tell them what you learned about responsibility this week.
4. Show what you learned by cleaning up afterwards!

Theme for the Week: Self-Control

Key Verse for the Week

Be hospitable, one who loves what is good, who is self-controlled, upright, holy and disciplined.

—*Titus 1:8*

Bible Reading: Titus 1:7-9

Under God's Control

Have you ever gotten so angry that you hit your sister or called your little brother nasty names? If so, your mom or dad probably asked, "What were you thinking? Why on earth did you do that?" And you probably had a hard time coming up with a good answer.

Out-of-control words and actions tend to spill out like a glass of milk accidentally tipped over on the dinner table. You don't usually mean to say or do nasty things, but sometimes you lose control! When you're angry or upset, it's hard to keep your cool.

Titus 1:8 tells us to "be hospitable, one who loves what is good, who is self-controlled, upright, holy and disciplined." Self-control is hard. But take heart—in God's strength, under God's control—you can control your thoughts, words, and actions.

So the next time your words or actions are spinning out of control, stop and pray. Give the problem to the Lord and put it under God's control. Replace your lost self-control with God's control of your life.

Something to Think About

During today's prayer time, ask for forgiveness for the times you've lost control of your words, thoughts, or actions. Ask God to put your life under God's control.

Dear Jesus,

I praise you for ______________________________

I'm sorry for ______________________________

I ask you for ______________________________

I thank you for ______________________________

Amen.

Sweet Surprises

Treat yourself and your family to a plateful of Sweet Surprises. Use self-control when you decide how many you'll eat!

What You Need

½ cup (.12 L) honey
½ cup (.12 L) peanut butter
1 cup (.24 L) nonfat dry milk
1 cup (.24 L) crushed cereal flakes

How to Do It

1. Ask an adult for permission to work in the kitchen.
2. Mix honey, peanut butter, and dry milk.
3. Form into balls.
4. Roll in the crushed cereal.

WEEK 2 TWO MONDAY ____________ (DATE)

Theme for the Week: Self-Control

Key Verse for the Week

Be hospitable, one who loves what is good, who is self-controlled, upright, holy and disciplined.

—*Titus 1:8*

Bible Reading: Titus 2:11-13

Living in Control

Just say no! is a popular slogan that reminds kids (and grown-ups) to say no to taking drugs. But it's a useful saying to remember in other areas of your life too. God wants you to say no to lying, stealing, jealousy, gossiping, cheating . . . and you can think of lots more.

Having the self-control to be able to say no to things that don't please God is only possible by God's grace. "For the grace of God that brings salvation has appeared to all. . . . It teaches us to say 'No' to ungodliness and worldly passions, and to live self-controlled, upright and godly lives in this present age" (Titus 2:11-12).

God's grace is the love and forgiveness you have through Jesus. You can't earn God's grace, and not one of us deserves it. God gives it to us freely because Jesus died on the cross for our sins and rose again. Because of Jesus, you can say yes to living a life that pleases God.

Something to Think About

Here's a saying to remember about grace: **G**od's **R**iches **A**t **C**hrist's **E**xpense. Isn't that great? You can experience all of the rich things God has to offer you because Jesus died and rose again for your sins. Praise the Lord!

Dear Jesus,

I praise you for ____

____

____

I'm sorry for ____

____

____

I ask you for ____

____

____

I thank you for ____

____

____ Amen.

Self-Control Through Grace Word Find

Find each of the words in Romans 16:20b. Remember that it's by God's GRACE (God's Riches At Christ's Expense) that you can say yes to self-control!

THE GRACE OF OUR LORD JESUS BE WITH YOU.

—Romans 16:20b

B	T	W	E	U	W	L	S	S	O	G	P	I
E	D	H	I	Q	S	P	W	K	S	K	U	M
E	K	Y	E	T	U	X	O	F	B	U	Z	Y
A	D	V	Z	E	H	G	P	Y	H	W	T	B
O	F	B	W	C	G	E	Q	B	J	T	R	R
V	W	Y	S	X	B	N	C	E	P	N	U	Y
K	K	S	W	P	V	W	I	E	P	O	Z	W
G	Z	X	G	T	P	P	H	V	C	J	K	F
T	G	T	F	L	F	P	J	Y	E	A	L	I
L	P	Y	Z	Y	U	P	O	S	L	V	R	A
P	S	W	H	V	U	U	U	O	L	T	D	G
N	N	N	L	P	B	S	R	S	P	G	Z	K
O	Q	F	H	Y	S	D	I	U	K	E	C	P

WEEK 2 TWO — TUESDAY ______
(DATE)

Theme for the Week: Self-Control

Key Verse for the Week

Be hospitable, one who loves what is good, who is self-controlled, upright, holy and disciplined.

—*Titus 1:8*

Bible Reading: James 3:7-10

Controlling the Tongue

Which of the following can't be tamed by people?

____ reptiles ____ the tongue ____ birds
____ animals ____ creatures of the sea

You can check your answer in James 3:7-8: "All kinds of animals, birds, reptiles and creatures of the sea are being tamed and have been tamed by man, but no man can tame the tongue. It is a restless evil, full of deadly poison."

The tongue can be like poison when you use it to tell lies, gossip, and swear. Without self-control, its poison can hurt families, destroy friendships, and ruin reputations. When God controls your tongue, your words can build strong ties within your family and bless your friends.

How can such a small part of your body be used for good and evil at the same time? It shouldn't! James 3:10 warns, "Out of the same mouth come praise and cursing. . . . This should not be."

Even your tongue needs to be under God's control. God won't accept praising and cursing coming out of the same mouth!

Something to Think About

Think of the last person you had a conversation with. Write his or her name here: ____________________ Who was in control of your tongue and conversation? Was it you or was it God?

Dear Jesus,

I praise you for ______________________________

____

____

I'm sorry for ______________________________

____

____

I ask you for ______________________________

____

____

I thank you for ______________________________

____

______________________________ Amen.

Fruit Dip (A tasty treat for your tongue!)

What You Need

Marshmallow cream
Your favorite fruit
8 ounces cream cheese (plain or strawberry flavored)

How to Do It

1. Ask an adult for permission to work in the kitchen.
2. Use a mixer to whip the marshmallow cream and cream cheese until light and fluffy.
3. Slice pieces of your favorite fruit: bananas, apples, oranges, grapes, pineapples.
4. Put your dip in a pretty bowl and set it in the middle of a plate. Arrange the fruit around the bowl.
5. Serve your fruit dish to your family. Tell them what you learned about self-control and the tongue.

Theme for the Week: Self-Control

Key Verse for the Week

Be hospitable, one who loves what is good, who is self-controlled, upright, holy and disciplined.

—*Titus 1:8*

Bible Reading: 1 Peter 1:13-16

Being in Holy Control

Have you ever felt like you were "set apart" from the rest of the kids in your class? Maybe you were the only person who forgot her gym shoes. Maybe you were the only person who got an A on the last spelling test. For better or worse, you were set apart.

God wants Christians to be holy and set apart from the rest of the world. As a Christian, your life should be different from non-Christians. Your goal should always be to please God, not yourself or others. God wants you, his daughter, to be holy and set apart from sin in all that you say and do.

Being holy requires self-control, hope in God's grace, and obedience. "Therefore, prepare your minds for action; be self-controlled; set your hope fully on the grace to be given you when Jesus Christ is revealed" (1 Peter 1:13).

Sitting down in the school cafeteria and praying before you eat takes self-control. So does trying to stop a group of kids from teasing a clumsy classmate. Although it's easier to conform to the ways of this sinful world than to be in God's holy control, nothing will be more wonderful than being "set apart" by God forever in heaven!

Something to Think About

God says, "Be holy, because I am holy" (1 Peter 1:16). Being holy starts with self-control!

Dear Jesus,

I praise you for ____________________

____

____

I'm sorry for ____________________

____

____

I ask you for ____________________

____

____

I thank you for ____________________

____

____________________ Amen.

No Cracking Up!

It's time to check who has the most self-control when it comes to cracking up and laughing!

What You Need

A friend or family member

How to Do It

1. Sit down and face your partner. You can sit across the table from each other or make yourselves comfortable on the living room floor.
2. Don't speak or laugh. (Making funny faces is permissible, though!)
3. Time how long it takes for you or your partner to lose self-control and start laughing.
4. Tell your friend or family member what you've being learning this week about putting your self-control under God's control.

Theme for the Week: Self-Control

Key Verse for the Week

Be hospitable, one who loves what is good, who is self-controlled, upright, holy and disciplined.

—*Titus 1:8*

Bible Reading: Galatians 5:22-23

A Wonderful Fruit

What kind of fruit does an orange tree grow?

___ apples ___ bananas
___ oranges ___ peaches

Didn't have to think too long about that question, did you? Obviously, the answer is oranges!

Galatians 5:22-23 talks about the fruit that should grow in a Christian's life. List the nine descriptions of this fruit and then circle the one that is our theme for this week:

__________ __________ __________
__________ __________ __________
__________ __________ __________

All nine of these things need to be evident in your life, including self-control. Does your family know you're a Christian by the way you control your actions? Do your neighbors and classmates know you love Jesus by the way you control your words?

When people see a tree filled with oranges, they know it's an orange tree. And when people see a life filled with the fruit of the Spirit, they know that person is a child of God.

Something to Think About

Our God loves to give good gifts. In your prayer, ask Jesus to help you grow the fruit of the Spirit in your life.

Dear Jesus,

I praise you for ______________________________

____

____

I'm sorry for ______________________________

____

____

I ask you for ______________________________

____

____

I thank you for ______________________________

____

______________________________ Amen.

Fruity Layer Cake

What You Need

1 piece of angel food cake (cubed)

2 tablespoons (30 mL) applesauce

1 cup (.24 L) large strawberries, hulled

1 medium kiwi

How to Do It

1. Layer cubed angel food cake in a clear water glass.
2. Spread applesauce on top of the cake.
3. Place strawberries on top of the applesauce.
4. Place the kiwi on top of the strawberries.
5. Make extras for your friends and family. Tell them what you learned about Christians and the fruit of the Spirit.

Theme for the Week: Self-Control

Key Verse for the Week

Be hospitable, one who loves what is good, who is self-controlled, upright, holy and disciplined.

—*Titus 1:8*

Bible Reading: Proverbs 16:32; Proverbs 29:11

Temper Tantrums

I have two sisters who are redheads. When they were small, kids in their class teased them by calling them "Carrot Top." There was a limit to how much teasing they could take, though. After that limit—look out!

You don't need red hair to throw a temper tantrum. People of all ages, sizes, shapes, and hair colors lose control of their tempers!

But God has a better way for us to respond when we're angry. It's called patience. "Better a patient man than a warrior, a man who controls his temper than one who takes a city" (Proverbs 16:32). It takes lots of self-control to be patient—"A fool gives full vent to his anger, but a wise man keeps himself under control" (Proverbs 29:11).

Do you have a nasty habit of throwing temper tantrums when things don't go your way? Do sharp, cutting words fly out of your mouth before you think about what you're saying? Once you lose control of your temper, it's hard to stop the flow of hurting words and actions. Keeping your temper under control is difficult, but in God's strength, you can do it!

Something to Think About

If you're struggling with temper tantrums, you've probably been told to slowly count to ten when you're angry. Here's a better suggestion: Ask God to bless you with patience. You can count on God's help to control your temper.

Dear Jesus,

I praise you for ______________________________

____

____

I'm sorry for ______________________________

____

____

I ask you for ______________________________

____

____

I thank you for ______________________________

____

______________________________ Amen.

Kazoo

Next time you lose your temper and your tongue gets you into serious trouble, make a kazoo and adopt this motto: Better to have my mouth playing a kazoo than out of control because of my temper!

What You Need

Fine-toothed comb

Piece of waxed paper

How to Do It

1. Fold the piece of waxed paper in half.
2. Wrap the comb in the fold with the "teeth" of the comb pointing out.
3. Place the back of the comb (folded between the wax paper) loosely between your lips. Hum a tune!

W E E K 2 T W O — S A T U R D A Y ______ (DATE)

Theme for the Week: Self-Control

Key Verse for the Week

Write the key verse for the week on the lines below.

______

______

______

—*Titus 1:8*

This Week I Learned . . .

Sunday
Being self-controlled with my words, actions, and thoughts begins by putting myself under God's control. (Titus 1:7-9)

Monday
I'm able to say yes to living a self-controlled life because of God's gift of grace. (Titus 2:11-13)

Tuesday
Without self-control, my tongue can be a poison that hurts others. With self-control, my tongue can bring praise to my Lord. (James 3:7-10)

Wednesday
Being holy and self-controlled sets me apart from the rest of the world. It may not always be easy, but I look forward to being "set apart" by God in heaven someday! (1 Peter 1:13-16)

Thursday
Christians need to have the fruit of the Spirit evident in their lives. Self-control is part of that fruit! (Galatians 5:22-23)

Friday
God wants me to use self-control and replace my temper tantrums with patience. (Proverbs 16:32; Proverbs 29:11)

Something to Think About

What area of your life needs improved self-control?

______

______

______

Dear Jesus,

I praise you for ____________________

I'm sorry for ____________________

I ask you for ____________________

I thank you for ____________________

Amen.

Monkey Bread

What You Need

1 package cook-and-serve butterscotch pudding mix
¾ cup (.18 L) sugar
1 tablespoon (15 mL) ground cinnamon
½ cup (.12 L) butter or margarine, melted
3 tubes refrigerated biscuits

How to Do It

1. Ask an adult for permission to work in the kitchen.
2. Combine pudding mix, sugar, and cinnamon in a plastic bowl with tight-fitting lid.
3. Pour the melted butter into a shallow bowl.
4. Cut the biscuits into quarters. Dip three or four pieces into the butter. Place them in the plastic bowl, put the lid on, and shake! Then place biscuits in a greased Bundt pan. Repeat this step with all biscuit pieces.
5. Bake at 350° for 30-35 minutes. Cool for 30 minutes then invert Monkey Bread onto a serving plate.

Theme for the Week: Self-Esteem

Key Verse for the Week

Don't you know that you yourselves are God's temple and that God's Spirit lives in you?

—1 Corinthians 3:16

Bible Reading: 1 Corinthians 3:16

Caring for God's Temple

If someone told you that Jesus was coming to your home for dinner, what plans would you make? Would you make a to-do list and have your whole family help? To start with, you'd probably want to clean the whole house (plus the garage and yard) and plan a special menu (no macaroni and cheese for Jesus!).

What a treat to have the King of kings and Lord of lords at your home for a special meal! You'd do your best to make your home beautiful and the food delicious. Your goal would be to have everything perfect for Jesus.

Although it's fun to think about having Jesus over for dinner, we won't actually see him face-to-face until we get to heaven. But if you believe in Jesus, the Bible has exciting news for you. Jesus doesn't have to come to your home for dinner to be with you. He's living in your heart right now!

The Bible says, "Don't you know that you yourselves are God's temple and that God's Spirit lives in you?" (1 Corinthians 3:16). If you'd make your home perfect for Jesus, shouldn't you do the same with your heart? So take good care of yourself, because your body is God's temple.

Something to think about:

You are one of God's special daughters. Does that make you feel good about yourself? It should! Always remember that you are God's temple, and your heart is God's home.

Dear Jesus,

I praise you for ____

____

____

I'm sorry for ____

____

____

I ask you for ____

____

____

I thank you for ____

____

____ Amen.

Word of the Week

To find the answer for today's puzzle, fill in the missing letter in each of the words found below. Transfer the letters to the corresponding numbered squares in the diagram.

1. DI ___ CIPLE
2. H ___ ART
3. TEMP ___ E
4. ___ RUIT
5. SP ___ CIAL
6. PRAI ___ E
7. SPIRI ___
8. DAUGHT ___ R
9. MARV ___ LOUS
10. TESTA ___ ENT

1	2	3	4	5	6	7	8	9	10

Theme for the Week: Self-Esteem

Key Verse for the Week

Don't you know that you yourselves are God's temple and that God's Spirit lives in you?

—1 Corinthians 3:16

Bible Reading: 1 Corinthians 6:19-20

Candy, Chips, and Coke

If you could choose a snack to eat right now, what would you pick?

____ a can of soda and a chocolate bar

____ a glass of milk and a fruit or vegetable

I know which one I'd pick—the soda and chocolate bar! Did I pick the one that was best for my body? Probably not. I picked what tastes the best to me.

Candy, chips, and Coke taste good—but they're not the best snack you can choose in order to grow healthy and strong. It's difficult to feel good about yourself when you're not taking good care of your body. Your body needs nutritious foods like bananas, green beans, and cheese to grow healthy and strong.

If you're a Christian, eating right, exercising, and keeping your body clean are not only good ways to take care of your body. More importantly, they're a part of living for Jesus. "Do you not know that your body is a temple of the Holy Spirit, who is in you, whom you have received from God?" (1 Corinthians 6:19) As God's daughter, you need to take the best possible care of that temple!

Something to Think About

Your self-esteem—feeling good about yourself—will grow when you take good care of your body. Think about the food you eat, how much exercise you get, and how often you bathe or brush your teeth. Are you taking good care of God's temple?

Dear Jesus,

I praise you for ______________________________

____

____

I'm sorry for ______________________________

____

____

I ask you for ______________________________

____

____

I thank you for ______________________________

____

______________________________ Amen.

Shape Up!

It's important to care for your body—God's temple. Pick a category that you have the most trouble with and set a goal for this week!

Eating

- Instead of reaching for can of pop, pour yourself juice, water, or milk.
- Replace your daily snack of cookies or candy with yogurt, cheese, fruit, or vegetables.

Exercising

- For 30 minutes a day, do one of the following:
  —jump rope
  —shoot hoops
  —exercise
  —walk or jog
  —swim

Cleansing

- Brush your teeth three times a day.
- Wash your face and hands often.
- Keep your body and hair clean.

Theme for the Week: Self-Esteem

Key Verse for the Week

Don't you know that you yourselves are God's temple and that God's Spirit lives in you?

—1 Corinthians 3:16

Bible Reading: Luke 12:27-31

Mirror, Mirror on the Wall

When you're standing in front of the bathroom mirror in the morning, rubbing the sleep out of your eyes, what's your first thought?

____ I hate my freckles.

____ I have cute dimples.

____ I love the color of my eyes.

____ I'm too skinny.

____ Other: ______________________________

Maybe what you see in the mirror doesn't bother you. Maybe it's more what you don't see in your closet. How often do you say to yourself, "I don't have anything to wear!"?

Relax! Being overly worried about clothes, hairstyles, and freckles, is what the Bible calls running after the things of this world. God made you just the way you are—dimples, freckles, and all. God also promises to take care of all your needs. He knows what you need before you even ask. He feeds the birds and clothes the grass. So how much more will he care for you, his child!

Often kids—and grown-ups too—judge themselves and others by how they dress and how they look. Their self-esteem is based on earthly things. God has a better plan: "Seek [God's] kingdom, and these things will be given to you as well" (Luke 12:31). Seek the things that really matter!

Something to Think About

Next time you study your reflection in the mirror, thank God for making you just the way you are. You're beautiful because you are a daughter of God! Remember that God always takes good care of his children.

Dear Jesus,

I praise you for ______________________________

I'm sorry for ______________________________

I ask you for ______________________________

I thank you for ______________________________

______________________________ Amen.

Here's Lookin' at You, Girl!

Ask your mom or dad for permission to temporarily "paint" around the edges of your bathroom mirror! Let it remind you that your self-esteem needs to be based on seeking God's heavenly kingdom, not the things of this world.

What You Need

Clear dishwashing soap (liquid)
Paintbrush
Premixed tempera paints
Muffin tin

How to Do It

1. For each color of paint, mix about 1 tablespoon of dish soap with ½ tablespoon of paint in the cup of a muffin tin.
2. Along with your own designs, paint the words "Seek first God's kingdom." Be careful to get paint only on the mirror!
3. To clean the mirror, wipe paint off with a moist paper towel.

Theme for the Week: Self-Esteem

Key Verse for the Week

Don't you know that you yourselves are God's temple and that God's Spirit lives in you?

—1 Corinthians 3:16

Bible Reading: Isaiah 45:9-12; Isaiah 64:8

I Want a New Shape!

Imagine that you're coloring a picture of a little girl who is sitting on a front porch swing reading a book. You pick out a black crayon and start coloring her hair. After you finish half of her hair, she suddenly gets angry with you. "Put that crayon down! I don't want black hair. I want to be a blonde!"

Pretty ridiculous, isn't it? It's funny to even think about a paper character arguing with its creator!

I wonder what God thinks when the children he created and designed complain or argue about their looks or talents. If you're like most of us, you've wished, at one time or another, that you were smarter, better at sports, or prettier. Maybe you've even told God that you want to be more like your best friend or your older sister.

Isaiah 45:9 says, "Woe to him who quarrels with his Maker, to him who is but a potsherd* among the potsherds on the ground. Does the clay say to the potter, 'What are you making?' Does your work say, 'He has no hands?'"

God made you just the way you are. And God never, ever makes a mistake. The color of your hair, the shape of your nose, the way you walk, your talents, and your personality were designed by the God who loves you.

*A potsherd is a broken piece of pottery

Something to Think About

Pots and vases come in all kinds of shapes and sizes. The clay doesn't say to the potter, "I want a new shape!" Make sure your attitude reflects your gratitude to God for your body!

Dear Jesus,

I praise you for ______________________________

____

____

I'm sorry for ______________________________

____

____

I ask you for ______________________________

____

____

I thank you for ______________________________

____

______________________________ Amen.

Be a Potter!

Time to make and mold your own clay. Your first project can be a small clay pot. Let it remind you of what you learned today!

What You Need

2 cups (.48 L) baking soda
1 cup (.24 L) cornstarch
1¼ cups (.30 L) cold water

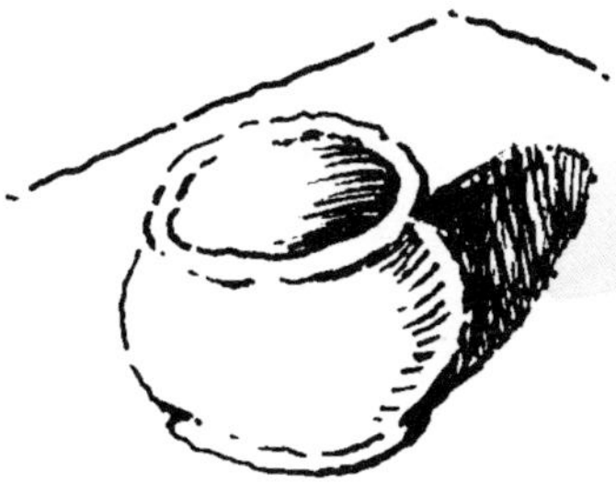

How to Do It

1. Ask an adult for permission to work in the kitchen.
2. Combine ingredients in saucepan until the mixture is smooth.
3. Bring to a boil, and boil for one minute.
4. Stir until it becomes the consistency of mashed potatoes.
5. Pour onto a tray and cover with damp cloth until mixture is cool.
6. Knead lightly. (optional: add a few drops of food coloring.)
7. Use immediately or keep in the refrigerator in an air-tight container. If refrigerated, warm to room temperature before using.

Theme for the Week: Self-Esteem

Key Verse for the Week

Don't you know that you yourselves are God's temple and that God's Spirit lives in you?

—1 Corinthians 3:16

Bible Reading: Psalm 139:13-16

Do You Have the "If Onlys"?

I know some girls who have a bad case of the "if onlys." Do you have this disease too? Whenever you think about your friends, do you begin your sentences with "if only"? If only I had a pretty face like Karisa. If only I had a different teacher. If only we hadn't moved.

If you've caught this sickness, don't worry. There's a cure! You can find it in Psalm 139:14: "I praise you because I am fearfully and wonderfully made; your works are wonderful, I know that full well."

God made you wonderfully. Before you were even born, God decided your height and weight, the size of your feet, and the length of your fingers. He knew if straight or curly hair would look just right on you!

God planned for you to be in your family, your school, your home, and your church. And God knows what will happen to you each hour of each day of each year until the day you go to be with him in heaven.

Something to Think About

Don't forget the first part of the Psalm 139:14: "I praise you because . . . " From now on replace all your "if onlys" with "I praise you, God." Here's how it works:

If only . . .

If only I had red hair instead of brown.

God made me wonderfully!

I praise you, God, for my brown hair!

Dear Jesus,

I praise you for ______________________________

____

____

I'm sorry for ______________________________

____

____

I ask you for ______________________________

____

____

I thank you for ______________________________

____

______________________________ Amen.

Baked Apples (You are the apple of God's eye!)

What You Need

2 apples

½ cup (.12 L) orange or apple juice

Filling:

1 teaspoon butter

Cinnamon (to taste)

2 tablespoons (30 mL) brown sugar

How to Do It

1. Ask an adult for permission to work in the kitchen.
2. Wash apples and remove the cores.
3. Stand apples upright in small baking dish.
4. Fill the center with filling.
5. Pour juice over apples.
6. Bake at 375° for 30-40 minutes until apples are tender when pierced with a fork. *Or* microwave on high for 4½ to 5½ minutes.
7. Serve warm or cold with juices from pan.

 FRIDAY ________ (DATE)

Theme for the Week: Self-Esteem

Key Verse for the Week

Don't you know that you yourselves are God's temple and that God's Spirit lives in you?

—1 Corinthians 3:16

Bible Reading: Jeremiah 29:11-13

What's the Plan?

Do you know what you want to be when you grow up? Maybe you've always known you wanted to be a teacher or a doctor. Or maybe your answer changes from year to year—beautician, business owner, or engineer.

As you grow, you'll ask yourself that question more and more. What do you want to be when you grow up? Many adults don't even know the answer yet!

You'll probably spend a lot of years praying and making decisions about your life. What career will you choose? Will you be single, or will you get married and have children? Where will you live? How will you be used to serve God?

Although you can't answer those questions yet, there's someone who knows all about you and all about your life—yesterday, today, and tomorrow. "'For I know the plans I have for you,' declares the Lord, 'plans to prosper you and not to harm you, plans to give you hope and a future'" (Jeremiah 29:11).

What's the plan for your life? God knows. Pray often. Give God your whole life—your today and tomorrow. God has a plan for you!

Something to Think About

Many times people don't think much of themselves because they have no hope. Praise the Lord that he "plans to give you hope and a future!" (verse 11).

Dear Jesus,

I praise you for ______________________________

I'm sorry for ______________________________

I ask you for ______________________________

I thank you for ______________________________

Amen.

Magnificent Me!

Doesn't it fill you with joy that God has a plan for your life? You have hope and a future! Celebrate God's plan for your life by making a Magnificent Me poster.

What You Need

Posterboard
Photos
Tape

How to Do It

1. Find your favorite photos of yourself. Try to find pictures of you by yourself, with your family, doing your favorite hobby, in your bedroom, and so on.
2. Across the top of your posterboard write "Magnificent Me!"
3. Tape or glue your pictures neatly on the posterboard.
4. Hang the poster in your room or on your refrigerator.
5. When other people see your poster, share with them your excitement that God has a plan for your life!

SATURDAY ______
(DATE)

Theme for the Week: Self-Esteem

Key Verse for the Week

Write the key verse for the week on the lines below.

______

______

______

—1 Corinthians 3:16

This Week I Learned . . .

Sunday
I can feel good about myself because my body is God's temple. What a privilege to have Jesus living inside of me! (1 Corinthians 3:16)

Monday
It's important to take care of my body, the Holy Spirit's temple, by eating food that's good for me, exercising, and keeping clean. (1 Corinthians 6:19-20)

Tuesday
My self-esteem must not rest on the things of this world—beauty, clothes, or hairstyles. I need to seek God's kingdom first. (Luke 12:27-31)

Wednesday
I shouldn't grumble about my looks. After all, God made me! Pots don't tell the potter that he made a mistake! (Isaiah 45:9-12; Isaiah 64:8)

Thursday
The "if only" disease can be cured by praising God. I thank God that I am fearfully and wonderfully made! (Psalm 139:13-16)

Friday
God has plans for me. My self-esteem is based in the hope and future I have with God. (Jeremiah 29:11-13)

Something to Think About

Have you changed the way you feel about yourself this week? In what way?

______

______

______

Dear Jesus,

I praise you for ____________________

____

____

I'm sorry for ____________________

____

____

I ask you for ____________________

____

____

I thank you for ____________________

____

____________________ Amen.

Popcorn & Pictures

What You Need

Bowl of popcorn

Your baby book and photo albums *or* Home videos

How to Do It

Time to gather your family around the photo albums or watch home videos. Share a bowl of popcorn with your parents and siblings. Ask your mom and dad some of the following questions:

1. What kind of baby was I? (Crabby, happy, content?)
2. What were you going to name me if I were a boy?
3. What dreams and hopes do you have for my future?
4. What did you want to be when you grew up?
5. What things do you think I'm good at?
6. I know that you love me, but why do you like me?

Theme for the Week: Relationships

Key Verse for the Week

Declare his glory among the nations, his marvelous deeds among all peoples.

—Psalm 96:3

Bible Reading: Psalm 96:1-3

Sharing Jesus with the World

Unless you live on a deserted island all by yourself, you have relationships with other people. People need relationships! It's been that way ever since God made Adam. The Bible tells us that when God saw that Adam was lonely, God made a woman, Eve, to be with Adam (Genesis 2).

Your relationships begin at home with your family members. You also develop relationships with people at school, in church, and around your neighborhood. Some of the people you know are a lot like you. Others are very different. And God specially handcrafted each person!

The world is full of unique individuals created by God. They use different languages and have different skin colors and nationalities. Yet there is one God who created, loves, and cares for them all!

Psalm 96:3 says, "Declare his glory among the nations, his marvelous deeds among all peoples." As a follower of Jesus, you should build your relationships—with family, friends, or neighbors far and near—by declaring God's glory and telling of his wonderful works.

Something to Think About

Most of us don't get to travel from country to country in order to tell other people about God's glory and deeds. If that's true for you, you can still build your relationships with people around the world by praying for them.

Dear Jesus,

I praise you for ______________________________

____

____

I'm sorry for ______________________________

____

____

I ask you for ______________________________

____

____

I thank you for ______________________________

____

______________________________ Amen.

Shaky Paintings

What You Need

Sheet of construction paper
Empty can with a lid (coffee, tennis ball, potato chip)
Tempera paint
Marbles

How to Do It

1. Roll up the sheet of construction paper and cut it so it fits inside your can.
2. Dip a marble into tempera paint and put it in the can.
3. Put the lid on the can and shake, shake, shake!
4. Carefully dump out the marble and wait a few minutes.
5. Optional: Take another marble and do steps 2 and 3 with a different color tempera paint.
6. Carefully pull out the paper. Look at the unique picture you made!

Theme for the Week: Relationships

Key Verse for the Week

Declare his glory among the nations, his marvelous deeds among all peoples.

—Psalm 96:3

Bible Reading: 1 Corinthians 12:14-20

Head and Shoulders, Knees and Toes

God created people with different personalities and talents. You'll never find two people who have identical strengths and weaknesses! Think of some of the people you know right now. List the names of your family members or friends that have these personality strengths:

Cheerful ________ Neat ________

Kind ________ Helpful ________

Giving ________ Good listener ________

Sometimes we become jealous of people. We wish we had their personality gifts ourselves. That's not God's plan for our relationships, though. God purposely gave each of us a different combination of gifts.

It makes sense. "But in fact God has arranged the parts in the body, every one of them, just as he wanted them to be. If they were all one part, where would the body be?" (1 Corinthians 12:18-19).

First Corinthians 12 talks about how Christians are the body of Christ. Each person has unique gifts or talents to use for the Lord. Each one represents a different part of the body—head and shoulders, knees and toes. A body with only one part is useless. The body of Christ needs each and every person. Your gifts are necessary to the body of Christ!

Something to Think About

What part of the body are you? List three personality gifts that God has given you.

____

____

____

Dear Jesus,

I praise you for ______________________________

I'm sorry for ______________________________

I ask you for ______________________________

I thank you for ______________________________

______________________________ Amen.

Body Part Word Search

These body parts are as necessary to your body as your gifts are to the body of Christ. Have fun!

ANKLE	HIPS
ARMS	KNEES
BACK	LEGS
EARS	MOUTH
ELBOWS	NECK
EYES	NOSE
FOOT	SHOULDERS
HAND	TOES
HEAD	WRIST

J	S	E	E	N	K	S	S	S	W
S	N	E	C	K	W	M	R	T	R
L	H	D	E	O	R	A	S	O	I
E	S	O	B	A	E	H	C	E	S
G	K	L	U	A	B	S	A	S	T
S	E	N	F	L	N	A	E	N	E
P	X	O	D	S	D	K	C	Y	D
I	O	A	F	J	P	E	L	K	E
T	E	E	S	O	N	I	R	E	L
H	M	O	U	T	H	K	H	S	D

Theme for the Week: Relationships

Key Verse for the Week

Declare his glory among the nations, his marvelous deeds among all peoples.

—Psalm 96:3

Bible Reading: 1 Corinthians 15:33

Good Friends = Good Character

Ever heard the saying, "You can choose your friends, but you can't choose your relatives"? Even if it's a little silly, it's true. You didn't get to choose your parents, grandparents, brothers, or sisters. You were born with them.

It's different with friendships. As you grow, you meet new people and make new friends. You probably have a best friend or a group of close friends you love spending time with. God blesses us with a wonderful gift when we enjoy the special relationship we call friendship.

Today's Bible passage gives a warning about our relationships with our friends. "Do not be misled: 'Bad company corrupts good character'" (1 Corinthians 15:33). The passage is telling us that bad friends = bad character!

So if your closest friends don't know Jesus, be careful! If you spend a lot of time with those friends, you may be in danger of losing your best friend, Jesus Christ. It's important to witness to friends who don't know Jesus. It's also necessary for Christians to have friends who love Jesus. Remember that the opposite of "bad friends = bad character" is "good friends = good character"!

Something to Think About

Is your closest friend a Christian? If she is, give her a call and tell her how important her friendship is to you!

Dear Jesus,

I praise you for ______________________________

____

____

I'm sorry for ______________________________

____

____

I ask you for ______________________________

____

____

I thank you for ______________________________

____

______________________________ Amen.

Bagel Butterfly

What You Need

Top or bottom half of a bagel
Gumdrops
Spreadable cream cheese (any flavor)
Licorice whips
Cake decorating sprinkles or candy

How to Do It

1. Ask an adult for permission to work in the kitchen.
2. Cut the bagel in half and turn outward to form wings.
3. Spread cream cheese over bagel.
4. Place candies or sprinkles on the cream cheese wings.
5. Attach the butterfly's head (gumdrop) to the wings with cream cheese.
6. Push 2 antennae (licorice whips) into its gumdrop head.
7. *Optional:* Invite your friends over and make Bagel Butterflies together. Tell them what you learned about friendship today!

Theme for the Week: Relationships

Key Verse for the Week

Declare his glory among the nations, his marvelous deeds among all peoples.

—Psalm 96:3

Bible Reading: Romans 12:9-13

Sharing with God's People

The Bible is filled with rules about our relationships with other people—rules like love your enemies, obey your parents, respect those in authority, live in harmony with one another.

One kind of relationship the Bible talks about is the relationship God's people have with each other. God's people are those who love the Lord and believe in Jesus. They may be Christian family members, friends, church members, or your classmates in church school.

Your relationship with God's people is so important to God that we find specific instructions in Romans 12:13: "Share with God's people who are in need. Practice hospitality."

God wants you to reach out and share with those who have needs. Just because people are children of God doesn't mean that their lives are perfect. God's sons and daughters have needs too. As God's child, you need to be sensitive to hurting people. You can be God's hands and feet by reaching out with the love of Jesus and sharing your gifts with others. It's one of the many privileges of being in the family of God!

Something to Think About

Do you know someone who is sick, sad, or lonely? Send that person a card, or cheer her up with a visit or telephone call.

Dear Jesus,

I praise you for ______________________________

I'm sorry for ______________________________

I ask you for ______________________________

I thank you for ______________________________

______________________________ Amen.

Relationship Chain

Celebrate your relationships with the family of God by making a paper chain. Hang it up as a reminder to pray for and help God's people.

What You Need

Colored paper
Pencil
Scissors
Ruler
Glue
Markers

How to Do It

1. Use a pencil to draw lines lengthwise down the sheets of colored paper. (Draw the lines a ruler width apart.)
2. Cut the paper on the lines. If you're careful, you can cut several sheets of paper at the same time.
3. On each strip of paper use your markers to write the name of someone who is in the family of God.
4. Stick the ends of the first link together with your glue.
5. Put another link through the first one and stick the ends together.
6. Keep repeating the steps until your chain is the length that you want!

Theme for the Week: Relationships

Key Verse for the Week

Declare his glory among the nations, his marvelous deeds among all peoples.

—Psalm 96:3

Bible Reading: Psalm 22:27-28

Lord of the Nations

If you grab a newsmagazine or watch the news tonight on television, you'll read and hear about nations fighting against nations. And if you glance at the headlines of your local newspaper, you'll probably read about hatred and violence right in your own town or a city near you.

God's perfect plan was for people to love one another and live in peace. But sin keeps destroying God's plan. Our world is filled with murder, hatred, and violence because people don't love others the way God intended.

It's easy to blame murderers and gangs for the hate you see in your country and around the world. But have you ever stopped to look in your own heart? Do you love your neighbors and the kids in your class the way God intended? Do you love the boy who has a different skin color than you or the girl who always smells bad? Do you love the unpopular kid or the lonely new girl the same way you love your best friend?

Think about your relationships with people nearby and across the world. Pray to the Lord of the nations for peace on earth. And put your hope and comfort in today's Bible verse: "For dominion belongs to the LORD and he rules over the nations" (Psalm 22:28). God is in control of your relationships! Let all peoples of the earth bow down and praise God!

Something to Think About

The next time you read or hear about nations at war or violence in your community, stop and ask the Lord of the nations to bring peace.

Dear Jesus,

I praise you for ______________________________

____

____

I'm sorry for ______________________________

____

____

I ask you for ______________________________

____

____

I thank you for ______________________________

____

______________________________ Amen.

"Stained Glass" People

What You Need

Brightly colored yarn
2 tablespoons (30 mL) white glue
Brightly colored tissue paper in a few colors
Newspapers
Scissors

How to Do It

1. Cover the table or area where you are working with newspapers.
2. Cut the yarn into several pieces, 12-24 inches in length.
3. Soak the yarn in the glue. Remove the excess glue by squeezing the yarn through your fingers.
4. Press the yarn to brightly colored tissue paper in the shape of a person.
5. Make several people. Dry thoroughly. With scissors, trim the tissue from the edges.
6. Hang the "stained glass" people in front of your window. Let the different colors and shapes remind you that God's love (like the sun) shines through all the people who love him.

Theme for the Week: Relationships

Key Verse for the Week

Declare his glory among the nations, his marvelous deeds among all peoples.

—Psalm 96:3

Bible Reading: Philippians 2:9-11

Bowing Knees, Confessing Tongues

If you stop to think about it, girls your age who live in other countries are probably different from you in many ways. The food you eat, the kind of house you live in, the size of your school, the way you worship in church—all these are vastly different from the way other girls live across the globe.

The differences between people in this world are more than we can even begin to comprehend. But although our day-to-day lives reflect our differences, there will be one day (we're still waiting!) when each person in every country across the world will be doing the exact same thing.

Philippians 2:10-11 tells of the event that will unify people from continent to continent: "At the name of Jesus every knee should bow, in heaven and on earth and under the earth, and every tongue confess that Jesus Christ is Lord, to the glory of God the Father."

How incredible! Someday Jesus will come back to earth, and one girl will lay down her chopsticks, another will leave her grass hut, another will quit rollerblading, and at the same time—all together—they will bow down and confess with their tongues that Jesus Christ is Lord!

Something to Think About

Are you looking forward to that day? I am! Pray with me, "Come quickly, Lord Jesus, come quickly!"

Dear Jesus,

I praise you for ______________________________

____

____

I'm sorry for ______________________________

____

____

I ask you for ______________________________

____

____

I thank you for ______________________________

____

______________________________ Amen.

Pole to Pole Word Puzzle

Match the numbers under the lines with the numbers in the globe. Write the corresponding words on the lines.

________ 12	________ 6	________ 9	________ 4
________ 1	________ 7	________ 3	________ 13
________ 11	________ 2	________ 10	
________ 5	________ 8		

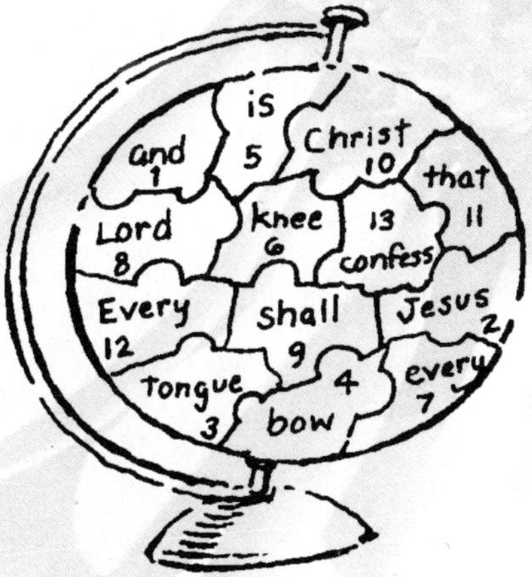

W E E K F O U R S A T U R D A Y ____________
(DATE)

Theme for the Week: Relationships

Key Verse for the Week

Write the key verse for the week on the lines below.

____

____

____

—Psalm 96:3

This Week I Learned . . .

Sunday
I need to have relationships with other people. All of my relationships should begin by declaring God's glory and marvelous deeds. (Psalm 96:1-3)

Monday
God created people with different gifts. Each person is needed to complete the body of Christ. (1 Corinthians 12:14-20)

Tuesday
It's important that my relationships with others include Christian friends. The Bible warns that "bad company corrupts good character." (1 Corinthians 15:33)

Wednesday
When it comes to my relationships with God's people, I need to always remember to reach out to those in need. (Romans 12:9-13)

Thursday
The Lord rules over all the nations! I need to pray for God's peace for people across the world. (Psalm 22:27-28)

Friday
I look forward to the day when every knee will bow and every tongue confess that Jesus Christ is Lord! (Philippians 2:9-11)

Something to Think About

Think of one relationship you will try to improve this week. Write down what you plan to do.

____

____

____

Dear Jesus,

I praise you for ______________________________

____

____

I'm sorry for ______________________________

____

____

I ask you for ______________________________

____

____

I thank you for ______________________________

____

______________________________ Amen.

Shiny Rainbows

People across the world experience the warmth of the sun, the light of the moon, and colorful rainbows after thunderstorms. Make your own rainbow (without experiencing a storm first!).

What You Need

A clear glass of water
A sunny window
A white sheet of paper

How to Do It

1. Place the glass of water on a window ledge in bright sunlight.
2. Lay the sheet of paper on the floor.
3. You'll see the colors of God's rainbow!

WEEK FIVE — SUNDAY ________ (DATE)

Theme for the Week: Joy

Key Verse for the Week

Be joyful always.

—1 Thessalonians 5:16

Bible Reading: 1 Thessalonians 5:16-18

Be Joyful Always

"Hey, Smiley!" That's how my dad used to greet me every morning when I was a little girl. Well, not *every* morning. He usually only called me Smiley when I was being grumpy! "Hey, Smiley!" was Dad's way of reminding me to put a smile on my face and be happy!

Being happy and being joyful are really two different things. Did you know that? Many people don't realize that there's a difference because they seem so similar. They both bring smiles to people's faces!

The difference isn't the width of the smile. The difference is where the smile begins! Happiness depends on your surroundings—things that happen on the outside. Which things make you happy? A fun birthday party? A surprise gift? A new outfit? These are all good things. But, like your memories of a family vacation, happiness always fades away.

Joyfulness, on the other hand, comes from the inside. You experience joy when Jesus lives in your heart. Joy doesn't disappear like happiness, because joy comes from having Jesus as your Savior. Only Jesus can bring true joy that will last for eternity into your life.

Something to Think About

First Thessalonians 5:16 says it the simplest and the best: "Be joyful always." You can be joyful *always* because Jesus will *always* be in your heart!

Dear Jesus,

I praise you for ______________________________

____

____

I'm sorry for ______________________________

____

____

I ask you for ______________________________

____

____

I thank you for ______________________________

____

______________________________ Amen.

Jump for Joy!

Time to find your jump rope and jump for joy! You can have a contest with a friend or family member or test your own skills. Have a jumping good time!

What You Need

A jump rope

How to Do It

Count how many times you can jump rope doing the various challenges!

Challenge #1: Jump rope your favorite way.

Challenge #2: Jump on your right foot.

Challenge #3: Jump on your left foot.

Challenge #4: Jump rope backwards.

Challenge #5: Jump rope with your eyes shut!

Theme for the Week: Joy

Key Verse for the Week

Be joyful always.

—1 Thessalonians 5:16

Bible Reading: Proverbs 15:30

Sharing the Joy

If you've ever had chicken pox or another "catchy" illness, you probably missed a few days of school. Maybe even a picnic with your cousins. When you have a contagious illness, people can catch your germs. So they stay away. They don't want to get your sickness!

Having a contagious illness is bad—it makes people want to stay away from you. But did you know that there's also a good way to be contagious? Joy is contagious. It starts in your heart. When Jesus is number one in your life, your heart will be filled with joy. The joy will escape from your heart into a cheerful smile and attitude. And a cheerful smile and joyful attitude are contagious.

The Bible says, "A cheerful look brings joy to the heart, and good news gives health to the bones" (Proverbs 15:30). You can share the joy in your heart by giving others a cheerful look (a big smile!).

Jesus gives the joy. And you can share the joy because Jesus lives in your heart. Make it your goal to share some joy with someone today!

Something to Think About

Sharing joy with others is an inexpensive, effective way to witness for Jesus. Be a contagious Christian and share your joy!

Dear Jesus,

I praise you for ______________________________

____

____

I'm sorry for ______________________________

____

____

I ask you for ______________________________

____

____

I thank you for ______________________________

____

______________________________ Amen.

A Joyful Quotation

Fit the letters of each column into the boxes directly below them. The letters may or may not go into the boxes in the same order in which they are listed. That's up to you to decide. Once a letter is used, cross it off the top half of the puzzle and don't use it again. When you're finished, you will find the joyful quotation by reading the boxes from left to right.

	E		A		E	S		T	A	E		O	U	S		I	N		H	S	T		H	E		W	H	
B	S	H	A	R	C	O	N	T	H	G	I	J	O	Y		C	H	R	I	E	R	I	A	N	A	R	T	O
		■		■											■										■			
■							■				■				■			■				■						■

Theme for the Week: Joy

Key Verse for the Week

Be joyful always.

—1 Thessalonians 5:16

Bible Reading: Psalm 100

Singing for Joy

When's the last time you broke into song because your heart was overflowing with joy? It probably depends on whether you love music! But whether you sing beautifully or a little off-key, God loves to hear you praising his name in song!

The psalms are filled with joyful songs of praise. One of my favorite is Psalm 100. Fill in the key words that relate to joy!

> *Shout for ______________ to the LORD, all the earth. Worship the LORD with ______________; come before him with ______________ songs. Know that the LORD is God. It is he who made us, and we are his; we are his people, the sheep of his pasture. Enter his gates with ______________ and his courts with ______________; give ______________ to him and ______________ his name. For the LORD is good and his love endures forever; his faithfulness continues through all generations.*

Sing joyful hymns and songs of praise in your church. Sing for joy when you prepare for school in the morning. Sing a song of praise while you're cleaning your room. Spend part of your prayer and Bible reading time singing your favorite Bible songs to the Lord.

Sing to Jesus a song of thanks for the joy he gives to your life!

Something to Think About

The next time you're singing a song of joy, check the mirror. Your lyrics will be more convincing when there's a smile on your face.

Dear Jesus,

I praise you for ______________________________

____

____

I'm sorry for ______________________________

____

____

I ask you for ______________________________

____

____

I thank you for ______________________________

____

______________________________ Amen.

Cheery Cherry Snacks

What You Need

- 1 (7 ounce) plain milk chocolate candy bar
- 8 large marshmallows
- 8 graham cracker squares
- 1 cup (.24 L) cherry pie filling

How to Do It

1. Ask an adult for permission to work in the kitchen.
2. Break chocolate candy bar into 8 pieces.
3. Place one candy bar piece on top of each graham cracker square.
4. Place one marshmallow on top of each candy bar piece.
5. Place two crackers on a microwave-safe plate.
6. Microwave on high for 15-35 seconds or until chocolate is melted.
7. Top each snack with 1 tablespoon of pie filling.
8. Repeat steps 5-7 with the other graham crackers.
9. Serve to someone who needs a taste of cheer!

Theme for the Week: Joy

Key Verse for the Week

Be joyful always.

—1 Thessalonians 5:16

Bible Reading: James 1:2-5

Joy and Troubles

The last time you were sick with the flu, received a bad grade on a test, or had a fight with your best friend, what was your reaction?

________ I wish I could go back to bed and start this day all over again!

________ I am so grumpy and miserable. I think I need chocolate.

________ Oh, joy! I'm sure God will use my troubles for my good!

My own first reaction to trials or troubles is usually a craving for chocolate. That's not God's plan, though. When we face trials, God wants us to be joyful! "Consider it pure joy . . . whenever you face trials of many kinds" (James 1:2).

Your first reaction to trouble should be joy. Let's keep reading to find out why. "Because you know that the testing of your faith develops perseverance. Perseverance must finish its work so that you may be mature and complete, not lacking anything" (James 2:4-5).

When you're face-to-face with an upsetting situation, God wants you to look on the joyful side of the problem. Because of this trouble, your faith in God will be tested. You'll have to lean on God harder and pray more. When you do that, you'll be learning perseverance. And when you learn to persevere, or never give up, you'll become a mature Christian. It's a joyful process!

Something to Think About

Troubles = Joy = Tested Faith = Perseverance = A Mature You! Isn't it great to know that there's a positive, joyful side to trouble?

Dear Jesus,

I praise you for ____

____

____

I'm sorry for ____

____

____

I ask you for ____

____

____

I thank you for ____

____

____ Amen.

A Joy-filled Word Find

How many times can you find the word "joy" in this puzzle?

J	O	Y	O	J
O	J	O	Y	O
Y	Y	J	O	Y
Y	O	J	J	Y
O	J	O	Y	O
J	O	Y	O	J

Theme for the Week: Joy

Key Verse for the Week

Be joyful always.

—1 Thessalonians 5:16

Bible Reading: Philippians 1:3-6

When you're telling your best friend about your new puppy or showing your mom the A+ you got on your history report, most likely you've got a smile on your face and joy in your heart! When people talk to others about things they care deeply about, their conversations are usually filled with excitement and happiness.

Should your conversations with God be any different? In your prayers, you talk to God (your Creator, Savior, first love of your life) about things you care about (praise, confession, asking, thanksgiving). Shouldn't your conversations with God be as filled with joy as your conversations with friends and family?

Paul prayed with joy when he talked to God about the church members that were serving the Lord and partnering with him in sharing the gospel. "I thank my God every time I remember you. In all my prayers for all of you, I always pray with joy" (Philippians 1:3-4). Paul was thankful and joyful that the Philippian church believed in Jesus and joined him in telling others about Jesus.

When you're excited about what God is doing in your life or in the lives of others, tell him! Be joyful in your prayers. God listens to every prayer you pray. And God loves to hear your prayers of joy!

Something to Think About

Prayer time doesn't always have to be a quiet time. It should also be a joyful time of singing God's praises and celebrating Jesus' love.

Dear Jesus,

I praise you for ______________________________

____

____

I'm sorry for ______________________________

____

____

I ask you for ______________________________

____

____

I thank you for ______________________________

____

______________________________ Amen.

Joyful Prayer Time

Focus on praying prayers of joy today during your prayer time.

1. Go to your favorite (but private) place in your home or yard. If it's nice outside, take a blanket and put it under a tree or in a quiet corner. Sit on the blanket and enjoy the beauty of God's creation.
2. Praise the Lord for the joy he brings to your life because ______________.
   Tell the Lord you're sorry for the times you're not joyful because ______________.
   Ask God to help you be joyful in a problem you're having: ______________.
   Thank God for the joy he gives you through ______________.
3. Finish your prayer time by listening to Christian music, playing a song on a musical instrument, or singing a song of praise.

Theme for the Week: Joy

Key Verse for the Week

Be joyful always.

—1 Thessalonians 5:16

Bible Reading: Psalm 28:7-8

Leaping for Joy

Knowing that Jesus lives in your heart should fill you with joy. So it's appropriate that today's Bible verses talk about your heart, Jesus' house, leaping for joy. "The Lord is my strength and my shield; my heart trusts in him, and I am helped. My heart leaps for joy and I will give thanks to him in song" (Psalm 28:7).

There will be days, though, when you don't feel like leaping for joy. . . .

- when your mom is sick in the hospital
- when you're fighting with your best friend
- when your pet dies
- when you keep trying to understand math, but you just can't get it

On those kinds of days you may feel more like having a good cry than leaping for joy. Let the writer of Psalm 28 give you hope. Begin by reading the first part of verse 7 aloud three times: "The Lord is my strength. The Lord is my strength. The Lord is my strength." Lean on the Lord, especially when things are tough. God is your strength!

Remember the part about your heart leaping for joy? Your heart is Jesus' permanent home. He never leaves you. He never goes off to work or on a vacation. He never goes to sleep or out to lunch. Your heart can always leap for joy because Jesus is always there for you!

Something to Think About

Put your hands on your heart and praise Jesus for his love. Thank him for giving you joy on the great and not-so-great days in your life.

Dear Jesus,

I praise you for ______________________________

____

____

I'm sorry for ______________________________

____

____

I ask you for ______________________________

____

____

I thank you for ______________________________

____

______________________________ Amen.

Indoor Volleyball

It's time to fill your house with laughter. Have fun leaping for the volleyball (or should I say balloon?)!

What You Need

Balloon, Masking tape
Streamers (or yarn or string, long enough to reach across the room)

How to Do It

1. Blow up the balloon. It is now a volleyball!
2. Your streamer, yarn, or string will be your net. Use masking tape (ask permission from an adult before you put tape on the walls) and tape it to two opposite walls.
3. Grab your favorite partner(s) and play volleyball. Count how many times you can get the volleyball back and forth across the net without it touching the ground. This game requires lots of laughing and leaping!

WEEK FIVE SATURDAY ____________
(DATE)

Theme for the Week: Joy

Key Verse for the Week

Write the key verse for the week on the lines below.

____

____

—*1 Thessalonians 5:16*

This Week I Learned . . .

Sunday
Happiness depends on outside events like birthday parties and surprise gifts. Joy comes from the inside because Jesus lives in my heart. (1 Thessalonians 5:16-18)

Monday
I should let the joy that's in my heart spill out in a contagious smile. Jesus gives me joy so I can share it with others. (Proverbs 15:30)

Tuesday
Singing for joy should be a part of each day—whether I'm in church or cleaning my room or spending time with God. (Psalm 100)

Wednesday
I can turn my troubles into joy when I remember that God is testing my faith, teaching me perseverance, and molding me into a mature Christian. (James 1:2-5)

Thursday
When I'm filled with praise and thanksgiving to God, I should always pray with joy. (Philippians 1:3-6)

Friday
My heart leaps for joy because my heart is Jesus' home. He promises that he will never leave me! (Psalm 28:7-8)

Something to Think About

What new thing did you learn about joy this week?

____

____

____

Dear Jesus,

I praise you for ______________________________

____

____

I'm sorry for ______________________________

____

____

I ask you for ______________________________

____

____

I thank you for ______________________________

____

______________________________ Amen.

Festive Pretzels

What You Need

½ cup (.12 L) chocolate chips
6 pretzel rods
Colored sprinkles

How to Do It

1. Ask an adult for permission to work in the kitchen.
2. Pour the sprinkles on a plate.
3. Melt the chocolate chips in the microwave for 20-30 seconds.
4. Dunk a pretzel halfway into the chocolate, then roll it in the sprinkles.
5. Lay the pretzel on a piece of waxed paper so it can dry.
6. Repeat steps 3 and 4 with the remaining pretzels.
7. Serve these Festive Pretzels to your family and friends. Share with them what you learned this week about joy!

Theme for the Week: Kindness

Key Verse for the Week

Make sure that nobody pays back wrong for wrong, but always try to be kind to each other and to everyone else.

—1 Thessalonians 5:15

Bible Reading: 1 Thessalonians 5:12-15

It's Payback Time!

When your best friend tells you that another kid in your class is spreading lies about you, what's your first reaction?

______ It's payback time! You immediately defend yourself by telling everyone that she is a nasty liar.

______ You privately talk with her and show her kindness.

Most girls would take this hurtful situation and pay back a lie with a lie. Getting even is part of our sinful nature.

God's Word speaks specifically to "payback time" situations: "Make sure that nobody pays back wrong for wrong, but always try to be kind to each other and to everyone else" (1 Thessalonians 5:15).

Receiving a wrong and paying back kindness is something Jesus did perfectly while he was on earth. Even when he was dying on the cross (which was definitely a wrong because he never sinned), he didn't pay back a wrong for a wrong. Jesus paid back kindness and forgiveness to the people who crucified him. It's true. Check it out for yourself in Luke 23:34.

Follow Jesus' example and pay back wrongs with kindness.

Something to Think About

Having trouble with payback issues? In today's prayers, ask Jesus for his help. He'll give you the strength to forgive and pay back wrongs with kindness.

Dear Jesus,

I praise you for ____________________

____

____

I'm sorry for ____________________

____

____

I ask you for ____________________

____

____

I thank you for ____________________

____

____________________ Amen.

An O"K" Puzzle

K is for kindness, the theme for the week. Beginning with the first K in the puzzle, cross out every other letter. (Every letter you cross out should be a K.) You'll discover God's advice for payback times.

KMKAKKKEKSKUKRKEKTKHKAKTKNKOKBKOKDKYKPKAKYKSKBKAKCKKKWKRKOKNKGKFKOKRKWKR

KOKNKGK,BKUKTKAKLKWKAKYKSKTKRKYKTKOKBKEKKKIKNKDKTKOKEKAKCKHKOKTKHKEKRKAKNKD

KTKOKEKVKEKRKYKOKNKEKEKLKSKEK.

—1 Thessalonians 5:15

Theme for the Week: Kindness

Key Verse for the Week

Make sure that nobody pays back wrong for wrong, but always try to be kind to each other and to everyone else.

—1 Thessalonians 5:15

Bible Reading: Proverbs 11:16

Kindness: The Key to Getting Respect!

People earn their reputation through their words and actions. If you only think of yourself, for example, you can get a bad reputation. Maybe you've heard a few comments like these about someone in your class:

She is so stuck on herself, she doesn't know anyone else exists.

Her head is so big, I'm shocked she can fit in the room.

Her motto is "Me, myself, and I."

The key to earning respect and having a good reputation is found in today's Bible reading: "A kindhearted woman gains respect, but ruthless [people] gain only wealth" (Proverbs 11:16).

It's difficult to find fault with a kindhearted woman or girl. What will people say about her?

She's gives of herself to others all the time.

She never thinks of her own needs, only the needs of others.

She's too kind. I wish she'd be mean once in a while.

It's silly to complain about someone being too kind, isn't it? Having people respect you because of your kindness is one of the marks of a Christian. Ask God today to help you earn a reputation for kindness.

Something to Think About

If someone watched a video of the things you said and did this past week, what reputation would you earn? Think about it!

Dear Jesus,

I praise you for

I'm sorry for

I ask you for

I thank you for

Amen.

Growing Kindness

Growing a reputation for being kind starts with today's words and actions. It doesn't end there, though. It takes many days, weeks, and even months to be known as a kind person. Let today's project remind you that although it takes time to grow kindness, the rewards are beautiful!

What You Need

Empty egg carton
Marigold seeds
Soil

How to Do It

1. Fill each empty egg compartment with soil.
2. Press a flower seed into each section of soil.
3. Water the seeds lightly and place the carton in a sunny window.
4. Patiently wait until the seeds become small green plants.
5. When the plants are large enough, transplant them to a larger pot or to a flowerbed outside.

Theme for the Week: Kindness

Key Verse for the Week

Make sure that nobody pays back wrong for wrong, but always try to be kind to each other and to everyone else.

—1 Thessalonians 5:15

Bible Reading: Isaiah 63:7

Telling of God's Kindness

Although I struggle with being kind, it's comforting and wonderful to know that my God is a God of kindness. The Lord is always watching over his daughters and sons with a fatherly love that is kind and compassionate.

Today's Bible reading is a beautiful testimony to God's kindness. "I will tell of the kindnesses of the LORD, the deeds for which he is to be praised, according to all the LORD has done for us—yes, the many good things he has done for the house of Israel, according to his compassion and many kindnesses" (Isaiah 63:7).

Make this verse your testimony too. Fill in the blanks by writing your name in the blanks:

> ______________________ *will tell of the kindnesses of the Lord, the deeds for which he is to be praised, according to all the Lord has done for* ____________*—yes, the many good things he has done for the house of* ________________*, according to his compassion and many kindnesses.*

Think of one kind thing God has done for you, and write it down as part of your testimony:

____

____

____

Something to Think About

Dedicate your prayer time to praising and thanking God for all his kindnesses. Ask God to help you tell others about these kind deeds.

Dear Jesus,

I praise you for ____

____

I'm sorry for ____

____

I ask you for ____

____

I thank you for ____

____ Amen.

Teddy Bear Treats

The next time you're with your friends, tell them of Jesus' kindnesses to you. Be sure to show them kindness by sharing these Teddy Bear Treats.

What You Need

1 package microwave popcorn
1 tablespoon (15 mL) cinnamon
1 tablespoon (15 mL) sugar
1 tablespoon (15 mL) cocoa
⅔ cup (.16 L) M&Ms
1½ cups (.36 L) bear-shaped vanilla graham snacks

How to Do It

1. Ask an adult for permission to work in the kitchen.
2. Pop the popcorn according to the package directions.
3. In a large bowl combine cinnamon, sugar, and cocoa.
4. Put popcorn in the bowl and stir well.
5. Add M&Ms and teddy bear snacks. Stir well.

Theme for the Week: Kindness

Key Verse for the Week

Make sure that nobody pays back wrong for wrong, but always try to be kind to each other and to everyone else.

—1 Thessalonians 5:15

Bible Reading: Proverbs 12:25

Three-Step Heart Check

You don't need to be a cardiologist (that's a heart specialist) to recognize someone with an anxious heart.

Use this three-step heart check to discover when someone has an anxious heart:

- **Stop.** You can't do a heart check unless you stop what you're doing and pay attention to the other person.
- **Listen.** Is this person's conversation filled with worry? Is he concerned for a sick parent? Is she worried about her friendships?
- **Watch.** How is he or she acting? Is she bubbly and excited or silent and withdrawn? Is he fidgeting with his hands or pacing back and forth?

If one of your friends or family members has an anxious or worried heart, there is a cure. And it won't require hospitalization or medication! The Bible teaches us a way to bring healing to an anxious heart: "An anxious heart weighs a man down, but a kind word cheers him up" (Proverbs 12:25).

Your kind words can bring healing to anxious and broken hearts. So stop, listen, and watch. Don't ever miss an opportunity to cure someone's anxious heart with your kind words!

Something to Think About

Write the name of someone you know who has an anxious heart: ____________________.

Make sure you give this person a dose of kindness today!

Dear Jesus,

I praise you for ______________________________

I'm sorry for ______________________________

I ask you for ______________________________

I thank you for ______________________________

______________________________ Amen.

Kindness Coupons

In addition to kind words, kind actions also heal anxious hearts. Create and design personalized Kindness Coupons for people in your family, church, and community.

What You Need

A blank sheet of paper or 10 notecards
Markers
Scissors

How to Do It

1. If you're using a sheet of paper, cut it into 10 coupons.
2. Write down some kind acts that you will do for others in exchange for the coupon. For example: babysit for 3 hours; bake 2 dozen cookies; do yardwork for 2 hours. If you like to draw, decorate the coupons with borders or small drawings.
3. Hand the coupons out freely!

WEEK SIX — THURSDAY ____________ (DATE)

Theme for the Week: Kindness

Key Verse for the Week

Make sure that nobody pays back wrong for wrong, but always try to be kind to each other and to everyone else.

—1 Thessalonians 5:15

Bible Reading: 2 Timothy 2:22-24

If You Can't Say Something Nice . . .

Does this ever happen in your home? You start to say something bad about your brother or a kid at school, and your mom says, "If you can't say something nice . . . " You finish her sentence with, "I know, I know—then don't say anything at all."

Your mom is absolutely right! The Bible puts it this way: "And the Lord's servant must not quarrel; instead, he must be kind to everyone, able to teach, not resentful" (2 Timothy 2:24).

Let's look more closely at this verse:

And the Lord's servant: That's you!

must not quarrel: Saying unkind words almost always leads to quarrels or arguments. That's not the way God wants us to communicate.

instead, he must be kind: Replace your hurtful words and harmful actions with kindness.

to everyone: You must be kind to *everyone*—not just your favorite friends or your grandma!

Sometimes being kind to everyone can be hard to do. (Especially when they do things that aren't nice!) But with God's help, you can do it. Whenever you're tempted to tell something not very nice about someone else, remember what your mother says: "If you can't say something nice . . ."

Something to Think About

Is it possible to be kind to people who do unkind things? Think of someone who makes it hard for you to show kindness. Then ask for God's help to be kind to that person. Spend your energy doing and saying kind things.

Dear Jesus,

I praise you for ______________________________

____

____

I'm sorry for ______________________________

____

____

I ask you for ______________________________

____

____

I thank you for ______________________________

____

______________________________ Amen.

Kindness Puzzle

There's nothing puzzling about kindness! Have fun discovering the truth in this puzzle. Change each of the numbers into letters.

A	B	C	D	E	F	G	H	I	J	K	L	M	N	O	P	Q	R	S	T	U	V	W	X	Y	Z	_
1	2	3	4	5	6	7	8	9	10	11	12	13	14	15	16	17	18	19	20	21	22	23	24	25	26	27

__ ____ ?
4 15 27 25 15 21 27 23 1 14 20 27 20 15 27 2 5 27 7 18 5 1 20

__ __ __ __ __ __ __ !
2 5 27 11 9 14 4

Theme for the Week: Kindness

Key Verse for the Week

Make sure that nobody pays back wrong for wrong, but always try to be kind to each other and to everyone else.

—1 Thessalonians 5:15

Bible Reading: Titus 3:3-8

The Kindest Person on Earth

It's test time. How are your actions and words measuring up to the Bible's standards for kindness?

Think of three kind things that you did or said this week. Then write them on these lines:

____

____

____

I hope it didn't take you too long to fill those lines! Let's suppose that you've done 100,000 kind actions and said over 100,000 kind words in the past year. That's an impressive list. But could you ever make a list of your kind words and actions that would be long enough to save you from your sins and earn your entrance into heaven?

Titus 3:4-5 answers that question best: "But when the kindness and love of God our Savior [Jesus] appeared, he saved us [died on the cross and rose again], not because of righteous things we had done [not even 200,000 or more kind words or actions], but because of his mercy."

Something to Think About

Make it your goal to have an impressive list of kind deeds and words—but not because you think it will get you into heaven. Go after your kindness goal to show God your thankfulness for loving you so much that he sent Jesus to save you from your sins.

Dear Jesus,

I praise you for ______________________________

____

____

I'm sorry for ______________________________

____

____

I ask you for ______________________________

____

____

I thank you for ______________________________

____

______________________________ Amen.

Kindness Tape

What You Need

Video camera or tape recorder

How to Do It

1. Ask an adult for permission to use a video camera or tape recorder.
2. Decide who you are going to surprise with your kindness tape (a friend, grandparent, parent, brother or sister).
3. If, for example, you picked your grandpa, ask your grandpa's friends and relatives (with the video camera or tape recorder playing, of course!) to say something kind about him or tell about a kind thing he did for them.
4. When you're finished interviewing, give the tape to the person you honored. Tell the person how much you love and appreciate his or her kindness.

Theme for the Week: Kindness

Key Verse for the Week

Write the key verse for the week on the lines below.

____

____

____

____

—1 Thessalonians 5:15

This Week I Learned . . .

Sunday
God doesn't want me to pay back a wrong for a wrong. I should pay back wrongs with kindness. (1 Thessalonians 5:12-15)

Monday
Being kind is the key to earning people's respect and having a good reputation. (Proverbs 11:16)

Tuesday
I thank and praise the Lord for his loving kindnesses to me. I will tell others about God's kindnesses too. (Isaiah 63:7)

Wednesday
When I stop, listen, and watch others, I can find out if they have anxious hearts. I can help heal an anxious heart with a generous dose of kind words. (Proverbs 12:25)

Thursday
The Bible says that I must not quarrel (or say things that aren't nice). Instead, I should be kind to everyone. (2 Timothy 2:22-24)

Friday
I can never do enough kind deeds or say enough kind words to earn my way to heaven. Only Jesus can save me from my sins. (Titus 3:3-8)

Something to Think About

Who are you going to show more kindness to this week? What are you going to do?

____

____

Dear Jesus,

I praise you for ____________________

____

____

I'm sorry for ____________________

____

____

I ask you for ____________________

____

____

I thank you for ____________________

____

____________________ Amen.

Mini Cones

It's easy to give a maximum amount of kindness by making and sharing Mini Cones with your friends and family. Don't forget to tell them about what you're learning this week!

What You Need

Baker's chocolate or white chocolate squares
Bugles (corn snacks)
Plain M&Ms

How to Do It

1. Ask an adult for permission to work in the kitchen.
2. Melt two squares of chocolate in the microwave or on the stovetop.
3. Dip open end of Bugles in melted chocolate.
4. Put one M&M on top of each chocolate-dipped bugle.
5. Place cones on wax paper so they can "set." Enjoy!

WEEK SEVEN SUNDAY

______ (DATE)

Theme for the Week: Patience

Key Verse for the Week

Be completely humble and gentle; be patient, bearing with one another in love.

—Ephesians 4:2

Bible Reading: Ephesians 4:1-2

I Want Patience and I Want It *Now!*

Rate your patience level with other people:

1	2	3	4	5	6	7	8	9	10
Not so good				Average					Great

Rate your patience level with yourself:

1	2	3	4	5	6	7	8	9	10
Not so good				Average					Great

Rate your patience level with God:

1	2	3	4	5	6	7	8	9	10
Not so good				Average					Great

If you're honest, you'll admit that it's often difficult to be patient. When a friend keeps asking you to do something you don't feel like doing, most likely you'll lose patience with her. When you're learning a new song on the piano or working on a complicated math problem and you just can't seem to get it right, it's easy to lose patience with yourself. Or when God just doesn't seem to be answering your prayers fast enough, you'll even find yourself losing patience with God.

If you want patience and you want it *now,* you can start by praying for it and by learning what God says about it. "Be completely humble and gentle; be patient, bearing with one another in love" (Ephesians 4:2).

Something to Think About

When it comes to rating patience, listen to this good news: God is always 100 percent patient with you!

Dear Jesus,

I praise you for ______________________________

____

____

I'm sorry for ______________________________

____

____

I ask you for ______________________________

____

____

I thank you for ______________________________

____

______________________________ Amen.

Painting Patience

What You Need

Paint ingredients:
- —½ cup (.12 L) vinegar
- —½ cup (.12 L) cornstarch
- —Food coloring

Paintbrush

Paper

How to Do It

1. Mix vinegar and cornstarch together.
2. Add food coloring very slowly (be patient!) as you stir until you reach a color that you like.
3. If your paint is too thin, add more cornstarch. If it's too thick, add more vinegar.
4. Paint a picture or paint the word PATIENCE!

Theme for the Week: Patience

Key Verse for the Week

Be completely humble and gentle; be patient, bearing with one another in love.

—Ephesians 4:2

Bible Reading: Colossians 3:12-14

Living with a Long Fuse

Have you ever watched the cartoon characters the Roadrunner and the Coyote on TV? During each show, the Coyote tries (and fails) to harm the Roadrunner. Sometimes he uses a stick of dynamite with a short fuse, and before he can get it out of his hand, it explodes—BOOM!

The Coyote then gets creative with dynamite that has a very long fuse. He winds it around mountains, through valleys, under bridges, and over trees. It's sure to work this time, he thinks. The Coyote lights the fuse and watches the flame burn its way to the dynamite. It goes around, through, under, and over, and usually ends up right where the Coyote is standing—BOOM!

What do the Coyote and the Roadrunner have to do with patience? Nothing! It's the dynamite with a long fuse that I'd like you to think about. God wants you to have a long fuse! Your patience with others, yourself, and God should never burn on a short fuse that instantly explodes!

Colossians 3:12 says it this way: "Therefore, as God's chosen people, holy and dearly loved, clothe yourselves with compassion, kindness, humility, gentleness and patience." You are one of God's holy and dear children. As God's precious daughter, obey God's Word by clothing yourself with the beauty and elegance of patience.

Something to Think About

How long is your fuse? (Be honest!)

___ Short ___ Average ___ Long

Dear Jesus,

I praise you for ____________________

____

____

I'm sorry for ____________________

____

____

I ask you for ____________________

____

____

I thank you for ____________________

____

____________________ Amen.

Trying Your Patience

Find the line that leads to the word "patience." Remember, be patient. This may take a while!

Theme for the Week: Patience

Key Verse for the Week

Be completely humble and gentle; be patient, bearing with one another in love.

—Ephesians 4:2

Bible Reading: 1 Thessalonians 5:14-15

Personalities and Patience

God created you—and each person—with a unique personality. Most personalities, though, fit into one of four categories. Can you decide what category describes you best?

The Leader: These people can quickly make good and wise decisions. Other people look to them for guidance. They sometimes can be a bit bossy, though!

The Organizer: You'll recognize these folks by their ability to efficiently organize closets and class parties. When things get too chaotic, people in this group can get depressed.

The Life of the Party: These are the people who have lots of fun. They love to be the center of attention and make people laugh. Sometimes, in their efforts to be entertaining, they exaggerate or stretch the truth.

The Friend: People in this group have lots of friends. They're easy to get along with and they're excellent listeners. On the other hand, these folks can be too laid-back—sometimes they sit and watch others do all the work.

Personalities and patience go hand in hand. When you understand the differences in people's personalities, it's easier to obey God's Word: "Be patient with everyone" (1 Thessalonians 5:14). Practice patience with everyone by recognizing their different personalities.

Something to Think About

Did you decide what personality type fits you best?

___ Leader ___ Organizer

___ Life of the Party ___ Friend

Dear Jesus,

I praise you for ______________________________

____

____

I'm sorry for ______________________________

____

____

I ask you for ______________________________

____

____

I thank you for ______________________________

____

______________________________ Amen.

Frozen Treat

What You Need

1 cup (.24 L) sugar

1 envelope unsweetened cherry (or your choice) drink mix

3 cups (.72 L) milk

How to Do It

1. Ask an adult for permission to work in the kitchen.
2. Stir sugar, drink mix, and milk in a bowl until the sugar is dissolved.
3. Pour mixture into a shallow freezer container.
4. Cover the container and freeze for 1 hour. (Be patient!)
5. Remove container from the freezer and transfer the mixture into a mixing bowl. Beat until smooth.
6. Transfer the mixture back into the freezer container. Cover and freeze until firm. Remove from freezer 20 minutes before serving. If you're patient, the taste will be worth the wait!

Theme for the Week: Patience

Key Verse for the Week

Be completely humble and gentle; be patient, bearing with one another in love.

—Ephesians 4:2

Bible Reading: Psalm 37:5-7

Praying and Waiting, Waiting and Praying

Do you repeat some of your prayer requests day after day? I do. Every morning I ask God to give my family safety and good health. I also ask God to provide whatever my family members need that day. It's easy to be patient for God's answers to these requests. By nightfall, I've experienced God's yes or no. I'm thankful to say it's almost always yes! Then I offer a prayer of thanksgiving for God's constant care and protection.

But I also have prayer requests that I've been praying for years and years, and I'm still waiting for God's answer. I'm praying for some of my friends who want to have a baby. I'm praying for a lady in my church who has cancer. And I'm praying for our country to stop abortion. For all these requests, I'm still waiting for God's answer.

The writer of Psalm 37 also had prayer requests that left him waiting for God's answer. "Be still before the LORD and wait patiently for him; do not fret when men succeed in their ways, when they carry out their wicked schemes" (verse 7).

Do you ever pray and wait and then wait and pray? Remember to be still and wait patiently for God. God is listening. God will answer.

Something to Think About

Write down a request that you are praying and waiting for:

____

____

____

Be still and wait patiently for God's answer.

Dear Jesus,

I praise you for ____

____

____

I'm sorry for ____

____

____

I ask you for ____

____

____

I thank you for ____

____

____ Amen.

Pick a Letter

To solve this puzzle, circle one letter in each box. (Use a pencil with a big eraser. You may have to erase your circles a few times until you figure out the correct letters to solve the puzzle!) When you read across the puzzle, the circled letters will spell out a familiar Bible verse.

B	J	C	E	I	S	R	T	I	A	L	M
L	P	E	A	N	M	D	D	S	K	N	O
O	H	M	W	Y	T	H	F	U	A	T	J
E	I	D	A	V	M	J	G	O	A	D	Z

Theme for the Week: Patience

Key Verse for the Week

Be completely humble and gentle; be patient, bearing with one another in love.

—Ephesians 4:2

Bible Reading: Colossians 1:10-12

Patience Power

Do you know anyone who spends a lot of time talking about getting in shape but never actually begins exercising? Or someone who always complains about his spelling test grades but never bothers to study the words?

This week you've been searching God's Word and discovering the importance of patience. Spending weeks and months learning how God wants you to live a life of patience is useless, though, if you never discover the power it takes to be patient.

If you're serious about following God's command to be patient, read today's Bible verse. Colossians 1:10-11 says, "And we **pray** [patience power begins by asking God for it in prayer!] this in order that you may live a life worthy of the Lord and may please him in every way: bearing fruit in every good work, growing in the knowledge of God, being strengthened with all **power** according to his glorious might so that you may have great endurance and **patience**."

God will give you the power to live a life of patience. Ask God to strengthen you with his power to be patient so that your day-to-day life will please him in every way.

Something to Think About

Remember the triple "P"s: Prayer, Power, Patience!

Dear Jesus,

I praise you for ____

____

____

I'm sorry for ____

____

____

I ask you for ____

____

____

I thank you for ____

____

____ Amen.

Mini Burgers

What You Need

1 box vanilla wafers
1 box mint cream cookies
Red frosting
Green frosting
White syrup
Sesame seeds

How to Do It

1. Spread red frosting (catsup) on flat side of vanilla wafer.
2. Place mint cream cookie (hamburger) on top of frosting.
3. Spread green frosting (lettuce) on flat side of another vanilla wafer and place it on top of the "hamburger."
4. Dip your finger in the white syrup and spread lightly on top of the "burger bun." Sprinkle sesame seeds on top of syrup.
5. Let the burgers set at least four hours before serving.

WEEK 7 SEVEN FRIDAY ________
(DATE)

Theme for the Week: Patience

Key Verse for the Week

Be completely humble and gentle; be patient, bearing with one another in love.

—*Ephesians 4:2*

Bible Reading: James 5:7-8

Waiting for Jesus

Check the things that are difficult for you to wait for patiently:

___ chocolate chip cookies that are baking in the oven

___ going to the dentist to have three teeth pulled

___ the first day of school

___ the last day of school

Sometimes it's difficult to be patient. One of the hardest things for Christians to wait for patiently is Jesus' return from heaven. Ever since Jesus ascended into heaven, people have been waiting for him to come back again.

The Bible talks about that kind of waiting in James 5:7-8: "Be patient, then . . . until the Lord's coming. . . . Be patient and stand firm, because the Lord's coming is near."

When Jesus comes again, there will be no more crying, no more pain, no more sin. When Jesus returns, there will be no more dentist appointments. Your teeth will be made perfect! *Everything* will be made perfect!

Until Jesus comes again, we need to be patient and stand firm in our faith. We need to actively tell others about Jesus and our love for him while we patiently wait for his return.

Something to Think About

What are you looking forward to most when Jesus comes back again?

____

____

____

Dear Jesus,

I praise you for ______________________________

____

____

I'm sorry for ______________________________

____

____

I ask you for ______________________________

____

____

I thank you for ______________________________

____

______________________________ Amen.

Personal Poster

What You Need

Posterboard (you pick the size!)
Markers, crayons, or colored pencils

How to Do It

1. Write your name in cursive.
2. With a different color marker, crayon, or colored pencil trace around the outside of the name.
3. Continue using different colors to outline your name until it reaches the edges of the posterboard.
4. Hang it in your bedroom and let it remind you of your commitment to obey God and wait patiently for Christ's return.

W E E K 7 S E V E N — S A T U R D A Y ________
(DATE)

Theme for the Week: Patience

Key Verse for the Week

Write the key verse for the week on the lines below.

____

____

____

—Ephesians 4:2

This Week I Learned . . .

Sunday
Being patient with others, with myself, and with God begins with asking God for patience in prayer. (Ephesians 4:1-2)

Monday
God wants me to live my life with a "long fuse"! I need to clothe myself with the beauty of patience. (Colossians 3:12-14)

Tuesday
By understanding people's unique personalities, I can learn to be more patient with them. (1 Thessalonians 5:14-15)

Wednesday
When I pray, I must be still and wait patiently before the Lord. God is listening, and he will answer. (Psalm 37:5-7)

Thursday
Through **prayer** God will give me the **power** to live a life of **patience**. (Colossians 1:10-12)

Friday
I look forward to (and wait patiently for) Jesus' return. Until he comes again, I will stand firm in my faith and tell others about my love for Jesus. (James 5:7-8)

Something to Think About

Write the name of a person you need to be more patient with. What steps will you take to be more patient with him or her?

____

____

____

Dear Jesus,

I praise you for ______________________________

____

____

I'm sorry for ______________________________

____

____

I ask you for ______________________________

____

____

I thank you for ______________________________

____

______________________________ Amen.

Stir & Serve Drink

Treat yourself to this delicious drink. After you've stirred it up, go to a quiet, private place to drink it. Think about a situation that causes you to lose your patience. How can you handle the situation better in the future? Ask God for his power to help you be patient.

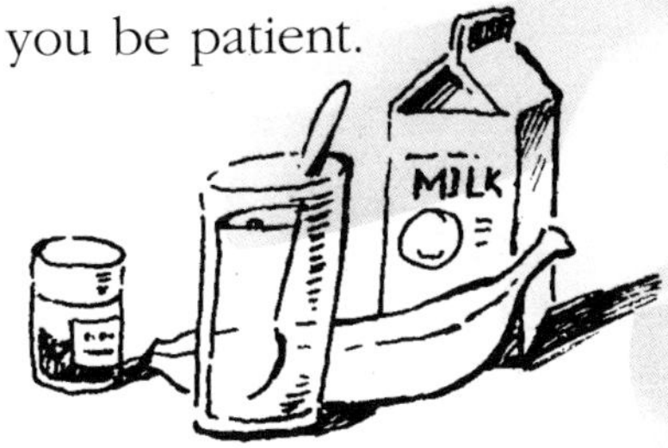

What You Need

2 scoops ice cream (any flavor)
2 tablespoons (30 mL) cocoa
1 cup (.24 L) milk
Dash of cinnamon
1 banana, broken into chunks

How to Do It

1. Ask an adult for permission to work in the kitchen.
2. Put all ingredients in a large glass and stir until well blended. (Or use a blender to mix ingredients.)

SUNDAY ________ (DATE)

Theme for the Week: Faithfulness

Key Verse for the Week

Let love and faithfulness never leave you; bind them around your neck, write them on the tablet of your heart.

—Proverbs 3:3

Bible Reading: Proverbs 3:3-4

What a Beautiful Necklace!

Many girls love to wear necklaces. How about you? Do you have a favorite necklace that belongs to you?

Whenever you're wearing a necklace (or any other kind of jewelry) that you received as a gift, you probably think about the person who gave it to you. Each time you look at it or touch it, you remember that person's love for you.

Today's Bible verse is about a different kind of necklace. "Let love and faithfulness never leave you; bind them around your neck, write them on the tablet of your heart" (Proverbs 3:3).

The psalm writer is using a word picture to help us understand what he means. Picture your love and faithfulness to God as a necklace that binds or encircles your life the way your favorite necklace encircles your neck.

Being faithful to God means consistently putting your faith in God each day. It means trusting God always and obeying him in every situation. Your love and faithfulness to God should be like a beautiful necklace that you never take off!

Something to Think About

Wear your favorite necklace (or ask if you can borrow one from your mom or grandma's jewelry box) this week to remind you what it means to be faithful to God.

Dear Jesus,

I praise you for ______________________________

I'm sorry for ______________________________

I ask you for ______________________________

I thank you for ______________________________

Amen.

Jewelry Box

What You Need

Plastic box with hinged lid (like a baby wipes box)
Felt squares (various colors)
Glue, Scissors, Fabric paint

How to Do It

1. Cut the pieces of felt just a bit smaller than the top and the four sides of your box. (For a unique look, use scissors with a zigzag edge.)
2. Glue the squares on the top and sides of your box.
3. Cut your remaining felt into three or four different shapes: circles, squares, hearts, flowers. Glue the shapes to the top and sides of your box.
4. Complete your jewelry box by writing your name on the box with a fabric pen or fabric paint.
5. Store your necklaces and other jewelry in your new box.

Theme for the Week: Faithfulness

Key Verse for the Week

Let love and faithfulness never leave you; bind them around your neck, write them on the tablet of your heart.

—*Proverbs 3:3*

Bible Reading: Psalm 89:1-8

Singing and Telling

Do you ever get goose bumps when you hear or see something that is really awesome? Every year when I watch my daughters sing and say their lines in the church Christmas program, I get goose bumps on my arms and tears in my eyes. Celebrating Christmas, along with remembering how God has been faithful to my family through another year, fills me with joy. I want to sing and tell others about the faithfulness of Jesus, my Lord and Savior!

I wonder if the writer of Psalm 89 ever got goose bumps when he thought about God's love and faithfulness. "I will sing of the LORD's great love forever; with my mouth I will make your faithfulness known through all generations" (verse 1). The psalmist sings and tells others about his awesome and mighty God. He praises the Lord for the wonders he has done. He declares that God's love will stand firm forever.

I'm sure that God has been doing awesome and wonderful things in your life too. Sit quietly for a few minutes and think only about God. How has God been faithful to you this week? How has he cared for you? Kept his promises to you? Showed you his mighty power? When you're finished thinking about your faithful God, sing a song of praise. Then go and tell someone else about God's love and faithfulness to you!

Something to Think About

After sitting and thinking about your faithful and awesome God, check your arms for goose bumps! Can anything be more awesome than God's faithful love to you?

Dear Jesus,

I praise you for ______________________________

____

____

I'm sorry for ______________________________

____

____

I ask you for ______________________________

____

____

I thank you for ______________________________

____

______________________________ *Amen.*

Word of the Week

To discover the key word of the week, fill in the correct missing letters in the words below. When you're finished, write the letters on the corresponding numbers under the puzzle.

1. POWER ___ UL
2. ___ WESOME
3. LOV ___ NG
4. MIGH ___ Y
5. ___ OLY
6. ___ ATHER
7. J ___ STICE
8. ___ ORD
9. FORGIVE ___ ESS
10. GRAC ___
11. KINDNE ___ S
12. RIGHTEOU ___

1	2	3	4	5	6	7	8	9	10	11	12

Theme for the Week: Faithfulness

Key Verse for the Week

Let love and faithfulness never leave you; bind them around your neck, write them on the tablet of your heart.

—Proverbs 3:3

Bible Reading: Joshua 24:14-15

Being God's Faithful Daughter

My friends have a beautiful stained-glass picture hanging in their home. The words of Joshua 24:15b are etched into the glass: "As for me and my household, we will serve the Lord." It's their family's testimony.

In order to live that beautiful testimony from verse 15, you need to read and obey verse 14 first. It gives us important how-to instructions: "Now fear the LORD and serve him with all faithfulness. Throw away the gods your forefathers worshiped beyond the River and in Egypt, and serve the LORD."

This verse should be easy to follow! Your bedroom is most likely not filled with "gods" of wood or stone. Since you haven't been bowing down to these "gods," you won't have any to throw away, right?

Wrong! Today the "gods" that we need to get rid of are the things that keep God from being first in our lives. Do you miss your devotional time because you watch too much TV? Do you spend more time playing video games than you do helping your mom or dad around the house?

In order to be God's faithful daughter, you must put God first in your life. When God is number one in your heart, you can testify, along with Joshua, "As for me and my family, we will serve the Lord!"

Something to Think About

Is there a "god" that sometimes becomes number one in your life? Write it down here:

____

Then ask God to help you give Jesus first place in your life.

Dear Jesus,

I praise you for ______________________________

____

____

I'm sorry for ______________________________

____

____

I ask you for ______________________________

____

____

I thank you for ______________________________

____

______________________________ Amen.

Peachy Shakes

Blend this peachy treat for your family. Read Joshua 24:15b to them and challenge them to make it your family's testimony too.

What You Need

1 cup (.24 L) buttermilk
3 cups (.72 L) sliced peaches
1 cup (.24 L) vanilla ice cream, softened
¼ cup (.6 L) sugar
¾ teaspoon (4 mL) ground cinnamon

How to Do It

1. Ask an adult for permission to work in the kitchen.
2. Put all ingredients in a blender; cover and process until smooth.
3. Pour into glasses. Makes 3 cups.

Theme for the Week: Faithfulness

Key Verse for the Week

Let love and faithfulness never leave you; bind them around your neck, write them on the tablet of your heart.

—Proverbs 3:3

Bible Reading: Psalm 100

Grandma, Mom, and Me

List these people that are on your family tree:

________________________ (you)

________________________ (your dad)

________________________ (your mom)

____

________________________ (your dad's parents)

____

________________________ (your mom's parents)

These names represent three generations of your family tree! The book of Psalms includes many verses that praise and thank God for his faithfulness to all generations. Psalm 100:5 is one of them: "For the LORD is good and his love endures forever; his faithfulness continues through all generations."

From the time God created Adam and Eve to the moment another baby is born, God's faithfulness to all generations continues. If you learned about Jesus through your parents and grandparents, you have a special reason to thank God for his faithfulness. The best family trees to grow on are the ones with generations of people who love the Lord and are faithful to him.

Something to Think About

Not every Christian grows up in a Christian family. If your parents or grandparents are not Christians, make sure that you say thanks to the person who first introduced you to Jesus as your Savior. Perhaps someday you will grow a Christian family tree of your own!

Dear Jesus,

I praise you for ______________________________

____

____

I'm sorry for ______________________________

____

____

I ask you for ______________________________

____

____

I thank you for ______________________________

____

______________________________ *Amen.*

Family Tree Find

Find some of the many relationships that grow on family trees!

- AUNT
- BROTHER
- COUSIN
- DAD
- DAUGHTER
- GRANDMA
- GRANDPA
- MOM
- NEPHEW
- NIECE
- SISTER
- SON
- UNCLE

U	B	N	I	I	E	N	M	R	A
B	D	R	O	I	L	O	E	U	P
S	E	A	O	S	M	T	N	R	A
N	T	L	D	T	H	T	U	E	P
I	L	T	I	G	H	T	H	T	D
S	M	W	U	N	E	E	R	S	N
U	W	A	I	T	W	L	R	I	A
O	D	E	I	K	U	T	C	S	R
C	C	W	E	H	P	E	N	N	G
E	X	A	M	D	N	A	R	G	U

Theme for the Week: Faithfulness

Key Verse for the Week

Let love and faithfulness never leave you; bind them around your neck, write them on the tablet of your heart.

—Proverbs 3:3

Bible Reading: Isaiah 25:1

Perfect Faithfulness

How faithful are you in serving and worshiping God? Put check marks by the things that you've done *perfectly* from the day you were born until today:

_____ Read the Bible and pray

_____ Help others

_____ Get along with everyone

_____ Obey parents

From the beginning of time, there hasn't been a single person (besides Jesus Christ) who can check any of the above items. There's never been a single person (besides Jesus Christ) who has ever remained *perfectly* faithful to God.

The writer of Isaiah praises the Lord because he is perfectly faithful. "O LORD, you are my God; I will exalt you and praise your name, for in perfect faithfulness you have done marvelous things, things planned long ago" (Isaiah 25:1).

God faithfully loves you, forgives you, cares for you, protects you—perfectly! Though we may sin and fail God, the Lord will never, never stop being faithful to us. Follow Isaiah's example and praise the Lord!

Something to Think About

Personalize Isaiah 25:1 by writing your name in the blanks. "O LORD, you are ______________'s God; ______________ will exalt you and praise your name, for in perfect faithfulness you have done marvelous things, things planned long ago."

Dear Jesus,

I praise you for ______________________________

____

____

I'm sorry for ______________________________

____

____

I ask you for ______________________________

____

____

I thank you for ______________________________

____

______________________________ Amen.

Pencil Holder

Pencils (with big erasers!) are another reminder that we can't always do things perfectly. Make a pencil holder to hold your favorite collection of pencils, or give it away as a gift.

What You Need

Magazines
Empty, clean soup can
Clear contact paper
Scissors
Glue

How to Do It

1. Cut positive words out of magazines. Examples: best, great, love, awesome.
2. Glue the words on the outside of the soup can.
3. After the glue has dried, cover the can with clear contact paper.

8

WEEK EIGHT — FRIDAY ____________ (DATE)

Theme for the Week: Faithfulness

Key Verse for the Week

Let love and faithfulness never leave you; bind them around your neck, write them on the tablet of your heart.

—Proverbs 3:3

Bible Reading: Lamentations 3:22-23

Great Is Your Faithfulness

No one can love you or be as faithful to you as God, your heavenly Father. Even though your parents love you dearly, there will be times when they break a promise or accidentally hurt you with their words. And even if you're the star student in your homeroom class, there will be times when even your favorite teacher will be unfair to you.

All sinners (parents, teachers, best friends—even you!) are sometimes unfaithful to God. Each time we do or say or think things that are displeasing to God, we are unfaithful.

But God is always faithful. God never breaks promises. He'll never hurt you or be unfair. God doesn't have bad days or ever accidentally forget about you. God has been faithful in the past. He is faithful today. And he'll be faithful to you tomorrow and forever. "His compassions never fail. They are new every morning; great is your faithfulness" (Lamentations 3:22b-23).

In an unfaithful world where people don't see the difference between right and wrong, God faithfully says, "I am the way." In an unfaithful world where people are lost in the darkness of sin, God faithfully says, "I am the light."

Something to Think About

Challenge yourself to do this tomorrow: Every hour on the hour (8:00, 9:00, 10:00 . . .), say a prayer of praise to God. Great is your faithfulness!

Dear Jesus,

I praise you for ______________________________

____

____

I'm sorry for ______________________________

____

____

I ask you for ______________________________

____

____

I thank you for ______________________________

____

______________________________ Amen.

Rainbow Toast

Rainbows remind us of God's promise to never again send a flood that would destroy the world (Genesis 9:14-15). Enjoy making and eating your Rainbow Toast, and celebrate God's faithfulness.

What You Need

¼ cup (.6 L) milk
3 or 4 drops of food coloring
Small, new paintbrush
White bread

How to Do It

1. Mix the milk and food coloring in a small bowl.
2. Use the mixture to paint a rainbow or other design on the bread.
3. Put the bread in the toaster and enjoy!

Theme for the Week: Faithfulness

Key Verse for the Week

Write the key verse for the week on the lines below.

____

____

____

—Proverbs 3:3

This Week I Learned . . .

Sunday
God's love and faithfulness should encircle my life like a necklace. (Proverbs 3:3-4)

Monday
Thinking about my faithful God makes me want to sing and tell others about him. It occasionally gives me goose bumps, too! (Psalm 89:1-8)

Tuesday
I can be God's faithful daughter when I get rid of other "gods" and keep Jesus #1 in my life. (Joshua 24:14-15)

Wednesday
God is faithful to the people in my family tree and all the generations from the beginning of time. (Psalm 100)

Thursday
I will praise the Lord because of his perfect faithfulness. (Isaiah 25:1)

Friday
Great is the Lord's faithfulness to me yesterday, today, and tomorrow. God is always faithful! (Lamentations 3:22-23)

Something to Think About

What did you learn about faithfulness this week that you didn't know about before?

____

____

____

Dear Jesus,

I praise you for ______________________

I'm sorry for ______________________

I ask you for ______________________

I thank you for ______________________

______________________ *Amen.*

Who Was God Talking To?

1. "Whenever I bring clouds over the earth and the rainbow appears . . . "

2. "I am the LORD. Tell Pharaoh king of Egypt . . . "

3. "Take your son, your only son, Isaac, whom you love, and go to . . . "

4. "Ask for whatever you want me to give you . . . "

Answers: (1) Genesis 9:8, 14; (2) Exodus 6:28-29; (3) Genesis 22:1-2; (4) 1 Kings 3:5.

Theme for the Week: Hope

Key Verse for the Week

We wait in hope for the LORD; he is our help and our shield.

—Psalm 33:20

Bible Reading: Psalm 33:17-22

Earthly Hope, Heavenly Hope

Hope is anticipating or wanting something that you do not have. Here are some examples of things you might hope for:

____ I hope we have a snowstorm so we won't have school tomorrow.

____ I hope that Jesus will come again soon.

____ I hope I get a CD player for my birthday.

____ I hope that I'll go to heaven someday.

Earthly hopes are wishes or dreams based on earthly things. Heavenly hopes are the promises that God makes in the Bible. Write an "E" by the things that are an earthly hope and an "H" by the things that are a heavenly hope.

Our wish for a snowstorm or a CD player may or may not come true. That's because hoping in things or people is always earthly hope—the kind that has no lasting guarantees or promises.

Christians have heavenly hope. That doesn't mean we never wish for good (or bad!) weather or a special gift. But our lasting hope is in God and God's promises. Only the Lord can give people a true and living hope. Psalm 33:20 says, "We wait in hope for the LORD; he is our help and our shield." Heavenly hope is guaranteed!

Something to Think About

Wishing for the things of this world—snowstorms or CDs—cannot help or save us. Only our Lord, the God we put our heavenly hope in, can be our help and shield.

Dear Jesus,

I praise you for ______________________________

____

____

I'm sorry for ______________________________

____

____

I ask you for ______________________________

____

____

I thank you for ______________________________

____

______________________________ *Amen.*

Hope Word Puzzle

Change the numbers into letters and solve this word puzzle that focuses on hope!

A	B	C	D	E	F	G	H	I	J	K	L	M	N	O	P	Q	R	S	T	U	V	W	X	Y	Z
26	25	24	23	22	21	20	19	18	17	16	15	14	13	12	11	10	9	8	7	6	5	4	3	2	1

14 26 16 22   2 12 6 9   19 12 11 22   26   19 22 26 5 22 13 15 2

19 12 11 22.   19 12 11 22   18 13   7 19 22   15 12 9 23!

Theme for the Week: Hope

Key Verse for the Week

We wait in hope for the LORD; he is our help and our shield.

—*Psalm 33:20*

Bible Reading: 1 Timothy 6:17-19

Looking for Hope in the Christmas Catalog

When I was a young girl, one of my favorite December activities was paging through the Christmas catalog. On almost every page I'd find something that I wanted or thought I needed. Each year I'd hope for bigger and better gifts under the Christmas tree!

I never received everything on my lengthy Christmas wish list. Most years, I got one or two gifts. And as I grew up, I discovered that putting my hope in things left me feeling empty. The things I wanted sooooooo badly would often break or get lost. Eventually, most of my "must-have" toys ended up at the bottom of the toy box or the back of my closet.

Some people still put their hope in the Christmas catalog. Others put their hope in money, good looks, intelligence, or athletic ability.

The Bible, though, warns us to put our hope elsewhere: "Command those who are rich in this present world not to be arrogant [proud] nor to put their hope in wealth, which is so uncertain, but to put their hope in God, who richly provides us with everything for our enjoyment" (1 Timothy 6:17).

Something to Think About

Do you spend more time hoping for things or hoping for Jesus to come again soon? Is your hope in the Christmas catalog or the Christmas baby?

Dear Jesus,

I praise you for ______________________________

____

____

I'm sorry for ______________________________

____

____

I ask you for ______________________________

____

____

I thank you for ______________________________

____

______________________________ Amen.

Frame Your Name

What You Need

1 sheet of black construction paper
1 sheet of colored construction paper (any color except black)
Glue, Scissors, Pen or pencil

How to Do It

1. Fold the colored construction paper in half lengthwise.
2. Write your name in cursive along the fold.
3. Cut around your name without crossing the folded line. (Also cut out the inside of the letters like the a, o, the loop of the l, and so on. Remember, don't cut over the folded line!)
4. Unfold your name and glue it on the black construction paper.

Theme for the Week: Hope

Key Verse for the Week

We wait in hope for the LORD; he is our help and our shield.

—*Psalm 33:20*

Bible Reading: Romans 15:13

Hope—A Gift from God

Is there any hope when . . .

- your mom tells your dad that she doesn't love him anymore?
- your best friend finds out she has cancer?
- your favorite uncle loses his job?

Maybe you're facing a situation that looks hopeless to you. Things may look bad today and even worse for tomorrow. If you're a Christian, there is even hope for your hopeless problem(s).

Ask God—through prayer—to give you hope. God promises to fill you to overflowing! Read this wonderful promise in Romans 15:13: "May the God of hope fill you with all joy and peace as you trust in him, so that you may overflow with hope by the power of the Holy Spirit."

You may have been through (or are going through) a sad or tough time that made you feel hopeless. Maybe the only thing that you felt overflowing was tears. It's OK to cry. God wants you to pour out your problems and aches to him in prayer.

After you've finished praying and wiping your tears, though, look up at the sky. The God who made the sun and the moon, the clouds and the heavens, will fill you with hope. God promised. Read Romans 15:13 again!

Something to Think About

Empty out your worries to God, and then let God fill you up again with hope.

Dear Jesus,

I praise you for ________________________________

I'm sorry for ________________________________

I ask you for ________________________________

I thank you for ________________________________

Amen.

Hope

Color the theme word for the week. Use markers, colored pencils, or paint.

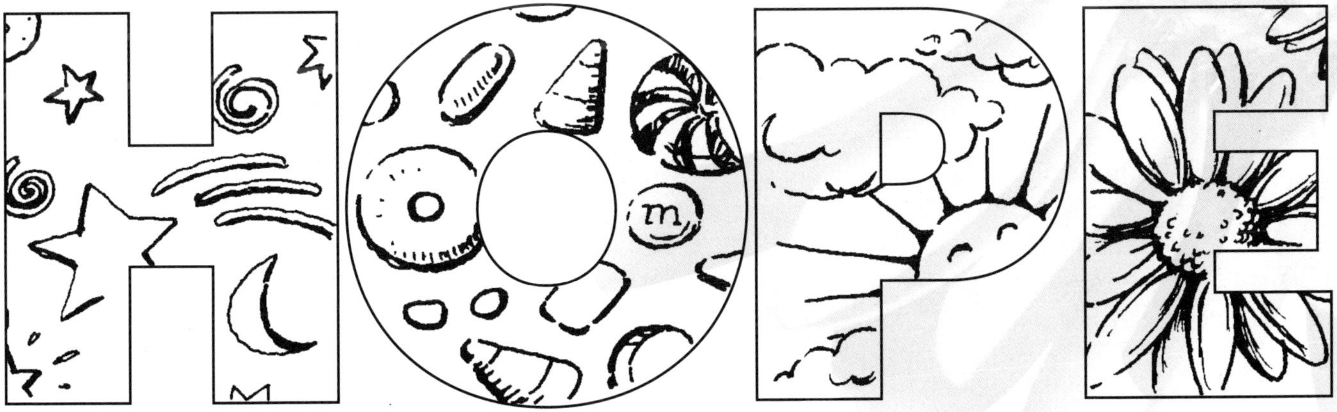

Theme for the Week: Hope

Key Verse for the Week

We wait in hope for the LORD; he is our help and our shield.

—Psalm 33:20

Bible Reading: Isaiah 40:30-31

Soaring Hope

Have you ever seen a mighty eagle soaring through the sky? Its powerful wings and graceful flight are an awesome sight you won't soon forget.

Would that eagle still be able to fly if its wing was broken? Of course not! It wouldn't be able to fly again until the broken wing was healed.

Sometimes we're like an eagle with a broken wing. We get tired, sad, or depressed. At times we stumble in our faith. We forget to have our devotions, or we hurt someone with our words. We sometimes fall into a bad habit that displeases God. When these things happen, we're living with a broken wing.

God invites us to go to him for strength when we stumble and fall. "But those who hope in the LORD will renew their strength. They will soar on wings like eagles; they will run and not grow weary, they will walk and not be faint" (Isaiah 40:31).

Are you having a "broken wing" day? Ask God to forgive you and renew your strength. Put your hope in the Lord and soar like an eagle.

Something to Think About

Find a book or website where you can learn more about eagles. Put a picture of an eagle by your bed and let it remind you to hope in the Lord and soar like an eagle!

Dear Jesus,

I praise you for ______________________________

____

____

I'm sorry for ______________________________

____

____

I ask you for ______________________________

____

____

I thank you for ______________________________

____

______________________________ Amen.

Bird Feeder

Make this bird feeder for your fine, feathered friends. Watch the birds enjoy eating your project, and let them remind you about what you learned today about soaring hope.

What You Need

Empty toilet paper roll, peanut butter, paper punch, 10" (25 cm) piece of string, birdseed

How to Do It

1. Punch one hole in the toilet paper roll near the top.
2. Punch a second hole directly across from the first one.
3. Tie one end of the string in one hole and the other end of the string to the other hole.
4. Spread peanut butter around the outside of the toilet paper roll.
5. Immediately roll the toilet paper roll in birdseed. Hang it in a tree.

Theme for the Week: Hope

Key Verse for the Week

We wait in hope for the LORD; he is our help and our shield.

—Psalm 33:20

Bible Reading: Psalm 42:5, 11

Hope When You're Sad

A couple of years ago we had a slumber party at our house. Eighteen giggly fourth-grade girls played games, stuffed themselves with pizza, and stayed up until the wee hours of the morning. The sounds of laughter rang through the house.

For many girls, life is full of laughter and fun. Christian girls rejoice in being daughters of God. Their smiles are a reflection of the love God has for them. Their attitudes show others that their hope is in the Lord.

But girls (and boys and adults) also have days when sadness wipes the smiles off their faces. When a grandparent dies or a parent has an accident, sadness fills our bodies. When your best friend tells a lie about you or you get a D+ on your science test, you probably get depressed.

Sometimes a day or two of sadness turns into a week or more of misery. When there are more tears than laughter in your house, the Bible has an answer for your sad heart. "Why are you downcast, O my soul? Why so disturbed within me? Put your hope in God, for I will yet praise him, my Savior and my God" (Psalm 42:5). Give your sadness to the Lord and let God fill you with hope.

Something to Think About

There are days when you'll be sad. There will be moments when you dread the next day because of your intense sorrow. When those days come, put your hope in God, who cares about your laughter—and your tears.

Dear Jesus,

I praise you for ______________________________

____

____

I'm sorry for ______________________________

____

____

I ask you for ______________________________

____

____

I thank you for ______________________________

____

______________________________ Amen.

Slumber Party Ideas

At your next slumber party, try one or more of these ideas:

- Give each person a white pillowcase to keep. Place a piece of cardboard inside the pillowcase and autograph each other's pillowcases with permanent markers or fabric pens. Each night when you go to sleep, you'll remember the fun time you had at your slumber party.
- Put fingernail polish on each other's nails with crazy patterns.
  —Cow pattern: First paint white, then put black spots on top.
  —Polka dots: First paint yellow, then put red dots on top. Or paint your school colors!
- Before the party begins, fill a jar with your favorite candy. (Count how many pieces of candy there are as you put them in the jar.) Have everyone at the party guess how many pieces of candy are in the jar. The winner gets the jar full of sweet treats!

Theme for the Week: Hope

Key Verse for the Week

We wait in hope for the LORD; he is our help and our shield.

—Psalm 33:20

Bible Reading: 1 Thessalonians 4:13-18

Heavenly Hope

If you've ever experienced the death of someone you loved very much, you've experienced the intensity of sadness that comes with death. Whether it was your grandparent, brother or sister, or one of the kids in your class, you know the ache that fills your heart because you miss being with that person.

If the person who died was a Christian, you have heavenly hope. "We do not want you to be ignorant about those who fall asleep [die], or to grieve like the rest of men, who have no hope" (1 Thessalonians 4:13). If that person believed in Jesus, you will see him or her again in heaven. That promise can fill your heart with hope and put a smile on your face!

What a wonderful joy it is to know that all Christians—from the beginning of creation until today—will one day live with the Lord forever (1 Thessalonians 4:17). It's awesome to think about living with Jesus forever!

Death also has a very sobering side that cannot be ignored. Those who do not have Jesus Christ in their heart as Lord of their life do not have that heavenly hope. If you want that heavenly hope for yourself, make sure that Jesus is your Lord and Savior today.

Something to Think About

Do you have friends or family members who don't know Jesus? Pray for them each day and tell them about Jesus' love.

Dear Jesus,

I praise you for ______________________________

____

____

I'm sorry for ______________________________

____

____

I ask you for ______________________________

____

____

I thank you for ______________________________

____

______________________________ Amen.

Peanut Butter Pizzas

What You Need

English muffins
Peanut butter
Optional toppings:
jelly, honey, apple or banana slices, dry cereal

How to Do It

1. Toast the English muffins.
2. Spread peanut butter on muffins.
3. Add your favorite topping or mixture of toppings.
4. Serve them to your family. Talk about someone who has died who your family misses. If the person was a Christian, share with them what you learned about heavenly hope. Tell them of the joy you have because death cannot steal hope away from God's children.

Theme for the Week: Hope

Key Verse for the Week

Write the key verse for the week on the lines below.

____

____

____

—Psalm 33:20

This Week I Learned . . .

Sunday

Hope is anticipating something that I don't have. When Christians hope in the Lord, they have a heavenly hope—it's guaranteed! (Psalm 33:17-22)

Monday

Putting my hope in the things that are in the Christmas catalog is useless. When I put my hope in heavenly things, God will richly provide me with everything that I need. (1 Timothy 6:17-19)

Tuesday

When I go to God with my "hopeless" situations, I'll be filled to overflowing with heavenly hope! (Romans 15:13)

Wednesday

When I have a "broken wing" day, I need to put my hope in the Lord. God will renew my strength and help me soar like an eagle. (Isaiah 40:30-31)

Thursday

When I'm sad, I need to go to God in prayer and put my hope in God. (Psalm 42:5, 11)

Friday

Death cannot steal a Christian's heavenly hope in Jesus Christ. Praise the Lord! (1 Thessalonians 4:13-18)

Something to Think About

Did you learn something new about hope this week? What was it?

____

____

____

Dear Jesus,

I praise you for ______________________________

____

____

I'm sorry for ______________________________

____

____

I ask you for ______________________________

____

____

I thank you for ______________________________

____

______________________________ Amen.

Hidden Rainbows

What You Need

Small sheet of paper
Crayons
Toothpick

How to Do It

1. Take your favorite color crayon and completely cover a small sheet of paper with that color. Press down hard!
2. Repeat step 1 with at least four other crayons.
3. When you're finished coloring, take a black crayon (press hard!) and cover the other colors.
4. Use a toothpick to scratch a rainbow design through the black layer of crayon. Do you see the rainbow colors? Give your picture to someone who needs to learn more about putting his or her hope in God.

10

W E E K T E N — S U N D A Y ________ (DATE)

Theme for the Week: Goodness

Key Verse for the Week

Nobody should seek his own good, but the good of others.

—1 Corinthians 10:24

Bible Reading: 1 Corinthians 10:24

Be a Goodness Seeker

When you graduated from crawling to walking, you probably started hearing these four little words: Be a good girl.

—"Be a good girl and don't touch that!"

—"Be a good girl and stay in here."

Being a good person is something you should never outgrow. That's because goodness is one of the fruits of the Spirit. All of God's children—young and old—should show this fruit in their lives.

When you were a toddler, you tried to be good to please your mom and dad. As you grow physically and in your faith, you'll want to make goodness visible in your life in order to please God.

God's children need to be goodness seekers—people who seek out ways to show goodness to the people around them. "Nobody should seek his own good, but the good of others" (1 Corinthians 10:24).

Being a goodness seeker is more than just avoiding a detention at school or not being grounded at home. It means constantly looking for opportunities to put the good of others before yourself.

Something to Think About

In the past twenty-four hours, whose good have you been seeking?

_______ your own

_______ other people's

Dear Jesus,

I praise you for ______________________________

I'm sorry for ______________________________

I ask you for ______________________________

I thank you for ______________________________

Amen.

That's Good Pudding!

What You Need

2 cups (.48 L) cold skim milk

2 tablespoons (30 mL) chunky peanut butter

1 cup (.24 L) light whipped topping

1 package instant chocolate pudding mix

How to Do It

1. Ask an adult for permission to work in the kitchen.
2. In a small bowl, mix 2 tablespoons (30 mL) milk and peanut butter until smooth.
3. Add ¾ cup (.18 L) whipped topping. Stir and set aside.
4. In a mixing bowl, beat pudding mix and remaining milk until blended (about 2 minutes). Let it stand for 5 minutes.
5. Spoon half of the pudding into six tall glasses or small bowls.
6. Layer the peanut butter mixture on top of the pudding mixture.
7. Add the remaining pudding.
8. Top all the glasses with the remaining whipped topping. It's good!

Theme for the Week: Goodness

Key Verse for the Week

Nobody should seek his own good, but the good of others.

—1 Corinthians 10:24

Bible Reading: Psalm 84:11; 86:5

Practice, Practice, Practice

The best way to learn how to play volleyball is by learning from an excellent volleyball coach and following the example of great players. Then, of course, you need to practice, practice, practice.

The best way to learn how to live a life of goodness is by learning from God's Word and following Jesus' example. Then, of course, you need to put into practice—practice, practice—the things you learned about goodness.

When we practice goodness, the Bible says, the Lord will bless us. "For the LORD God is a sun and shield; the LORD bestows favor and honor; no good thing does he withhold from those whose walk is blameless" (Psalm 84:11).

You may not always feel good about your own actions and words when you learn about God's perfect goodness. If that happens, remember the first part of Psalm 86:5: "You are forgiving and good, O Lord." After you've said or done some not-so-good things, go to God and ask for forgiveness. God promises to forgive you if you ask.

Our God is the goodness-giver. You can learn how to give God's goodness to others too. Keep learning about goodness in the Bible, and keep following God's example. Practice, practice, practice!

Something to Think About

Look in the book of Psalms. How many verses can you find that mention God's goodness?

____

Dear Jesus,

I praise you for ______________________________

____

____

I'm sorry for ______________________________

____

____

I ask you for ______________________________

____

____

I thank you for ______________________________

____

______________________________ Amen.

A Good Time Collage

What You Need

Notecards (or slips of paper)
Glue, Pens, Scissors
Construction paper
Your church school class, a church club, or a group of friends

How to Do It

1. Give each person in your group a pen and a set of notecards (as many as the number of kids in the group).
2. Write down a person's name on one side and something good about him or her on the other side. Example: *Diane. She always laughs and makes me feel good about myself.* Do this for each person.
3. Collect the notecards and sort them. Give each person his or her own "stack."
4. Read them out loud. Have fun receiving good compliments!
5. Cut the construction paper into a shape of something that you like (heart, rainbow, CD, candy bar). Glue your cards (with your name towards the back!) collage style on your shape. Hang it in your room.

Theme for the Week: Goodness

Key Verse for the Week

Nobody should seek his own good, but the good of others.

—1 Corinthians 10:24

Bible Reading: Luke 6:27-31

The Golden Rule

"Do to others as you would have them do to you" is called the Golden Rule. It's a rule that many people try to live by each day in their relationships with other people. But treating others the way we want to be treated is more than just a good idea—it's a rule Jesus taught to his disciples in Luke 6:31.

The Golden Rule is one of Jesus' many teachings on how we should show goodness to other people. Here are some others:

- Love your enemies (Luke 6:27a).
- Do good to those who hate you (Luke 6:27b).
- Pray for those who mistreat you (Luke 6:28b).

Many people—non-Christians as well as Christians—live the Golden Rule in their relationships with their friends and family. It's not too hard for us to treat the ones we love the way we want to be treated ourselves.

The hard part is applying Jesus' teachings about loving others to those who hate and mistreat us. For Christians, having a heart of goodness means applying the Golden Rule to *all* people—even our enemies. That includes the bully on the playground, the kid who tells lies about someone else to make them look bad . . . or anyone you just plain don't like.

Something to Think About

Is there someone you know who makes it hard to follow the Golden Rule? Write his or her name in the blank. Then pray for God's help in showing goodness to that person.

I will do to ______________ as I would have him/her do to me.

Dear Jesus,

I praise you for ______________________________

____

____

I'm sorry for ______________________________

____

____

I ask you for ______________________________

____

____

I thank you for ______________________________

____

______________________________ Amen.

Goodness

Color the theme word for the week. Use markers, colored pencils, or paints.

WEDNESDAY ____________
(DATE)

Theme for the Week: Goodness

Key Verse for the Week

Nobody should seek his own good, but the good of others.

—1 Corinthians 10:24

Bible Reading: Galatians 6:9-10

Are You Sick of Being Good?

Can you think of someone who doesn't know Jesus as his or her Savior and friend? Write the person's name on the blank: ____________________. One of the ways you can witness to this person is by showing him or her goodness.

If you wrote the name of someone in your class at school, you can spend extra time talking to her. Ask how her day is going, what she's going to do tonight, how much homework she has. Always use good and kind words. Let her see Jesus' goodness in your caring conversations.

If the person you wrote down is one of your neighbors, show him goodness through your actions. Ask him to shoot hoops. Volunteer to help him baby-sit his baby sister. Let him see Jesus' goodness in your actions.

After you've done these things for six months, a year, or maybe even longer, you might get sick of being "good," especially if your school friend or neighbor still wants nothing to do with Jesus. If he begins teasing you about your faith, you'll probably be tempted to quit being good to him.

When that happens, read Galatians 6:9: "Let us not become weary in doing good, for at the proper time we will reap a harvest if we do not give up." Jesus is watching your good words and actions. He will bless your efforts, and you will be rewarded.

Something to Think About

When you're having a hard time showing Jesus' goodness to someone, always remember that Jesus never gets sick of being good to you!

Dear Jesus,

I praise you for ______________________________

____

____

I'm sorry for ______________________________

____

____

I ask you for ______________________________

____

____

I thank you for ______________________________

____

______________________________ Amen.

A Goodness Quote

Fit the letters of each column into the boxes directly below them. The letters may or may not go into the boxes in the same order in which they are listed. You decide! Once a letter is used, cross it off the top half of the puzzle and don't use it again. When you're finished, you will find a Bible quotation about goodness by reading the boxes from left to right.

L	O	■	■	C	E	■	F	O	■	G	O	O	■	■	F	■	■	E	L	L	■	O	■	R	P	■	■	■	■
T	S	T	E	H	I	■	L	A	Y	I	T	Y	■	T	H	O	B	E	L	W	H	P	E	B	E	L	O	■	■
E	E	P	T	U	S	A	D	L	M	■	L	O	D	O	T	O	S	A	■	I	E	V	E	O	S	L	E	N	G
			■			■			■					■			■				■							■	■
										■			■						■				■						
		■				■							■			■										■	■	■	■

THURSDAY ________
(DATE)

Theme for the Week: Goodness

Key Verse for the Week

Nobody should seek his own good, but the good of others.

—1 Corinthians 10:24

Bible Reading: 1 Timothy 6:18-19

Rich or Poor?

When you think of being rich, what comes to your mind first?

_____ A home with six bedrooms, four baths, a three-car garage, and an indoor swimming pool?

_____ A top-of-the line Porsche with a leather interior?

_____ Name-brand shoes, name-brand jeans—yes, even name-brand underwear?

_____ A person who is always doing good deeds?

People who put material things like money, expensive clothing, and electronic toys as high priorities in their lives would probably choose one of the first three items on the list.

The Bible, on the other hand, associates being rich with people who are generous with their good deeds. "Command them to do good, to be rich in good deeds, and to be generous and willing to share" (1 Timothy 6:18). God wants you to share goodness with others as abundantly as God gives it to you.

Fortunately, being rich in good deeds doesn't necessarily mean purchasing expensive presents! Most of us don't have lots of money. Isn't it great that you don't need money to help clean your sister's room, or to rake leaves off your neighbor's yard, or to sing in the children's choir at church? All you need is a heart that is ready to do good for God's glory.

Something to Think About

Think about your actions in the past twenty-four hours. How would you rate your deeds?

1 2 3 4 5 6 7 8 9 10
Poor Rich

Dear Jesus,

I praise you for ______________________________

____

____

I'm sorry for ______________________________

____

____

I ask you for ______________________________

____

____

I thank you for ______________________________

____

______________________________ Amen.

Extra-Good Fruit Dip

Try this extra-good dip (complete with sprinkles) with your favorite fruits. Share it with your family tonight and tell them what you're learning about goodness this week.

What You Need

1½ cups (.36 L) strawberry yogurt
1½ cups (.36 L) whipped topping
¼ (.6 L) cup colored sprinkles
Your favorite fruits (apples, strawberries, grapes, and so on)

How to Do It

1. In a bowl, mix the yogurt, whipped topping, and half of the sprinkles.
2. Cover and refrigerate for 20 minutes.
3. Just before you serve the dip with the fruit, top with the remaining sprinkles. Mmmm, good!

Theme for the Week: Goodness

Key Verse for the Week

Nobody should seek his own good, but the good of others.

—1 Corinthians 10:24

Bible Reading: Romans 7:18-20, 24-25

Good Versus Evil—And the Winner Is . . .

Do you ever feel as if there's a battle between good and evil going on in your body? Maybe you can relate to this scenario: On Sunday night you decide that you're going to be extra good and help your mom or dad do the breakfast dishes every morning.

- Monday morning: You oversleep and are running late. It's a good thing you never told your mom or dad that you were going to help, because now you've run out of time. You promise yourself you'll do it tomorrow.
- Tuesday morning: You wake up extra early to wash the dishes. But when you walk into the kitchen, you see the sink overflowing with dirty dishes. Yuck! I'll start tomorrow, you tell yourself.

On and on it goes. You want to do good, but you always tend to choose evil. You're not alone if you've ever felt that way. The apostle Paul had the same problem. He wrote, "For what I do is not the good I want to do; no, the evil I do not want to do—this I keep on doing" (Romans 7:19).

If you're discouraged that evil always seems to be the winner over good in your life, there's hope. In verses 24 and 25 Paul wonders who will rescue him from this problem. The answer (for Paul and for you!) is Jesus Christ our Lord. Thanks be to him for being the winner over evil!

Something to Think About

In the war between good and evil, the winner is . . . Jesus Christ! The victory always belongs to the Lord.

Dear Jesus,

I praise you for ______________________________

____

____

I'm sorry for ______________________________

____

____

I ask you for ______________________________

____

____

I thank you for ______________________________

____

______________________________ Amen.

Find the Goodness

WEEK TEN — SATURDAY ________ (DATE)

Theme for the Week: Goodness

Key Verse for the Week

Write the key verse for the week on the lines below.

____

____

—1 Corinthians 10:24

This Week I Learned . . .

Sunday
Being good is something I should never outgrow. I need to be a goodness seeker, always seeking the good of others instead of my own good. (1 Corinthians 10:24)

Monday
In order to live a life of goodness, I need to learn about goodness in the Bible, follow Jesus' example, and practice, practice, practice. (Psalm 84:11; 86:5)

Tuesday
The Golden Rule is more than just a nice suggestion for the world. God expects me to treat others as I would have them treat me. That includes my friends *and* enemies! (Luke 6:27-31)

Wednesday
My goodness to others is a witness to the goodness that Jesus gives to me. Plus, I'm promised a heavenly reward! (Galatians 6:9-10)

Thursday
To God, being rich has nothing to do with six-bedroom homes or brand-name jeans. God wants me to be rich in good deeds. (1 Timothy 6:18-19)

Friday
Jesus Christ is Lord (and the winner!) in the battle that goes on in my life between good and evil. (Romans 7:18-20, 24-25)

Something to Think About

How are you going to show Jesus' goodness to others this week?

____

____

Dear Jesus,

I praise you for ______________________________

____

____

I'm sorry for ______________________________

____

____

I ask you for ______________________________

____

____

I thank you for ______________________________

____

______________________________ Amen.

Goodness Box

What You Need

A shoebox
Markers, pencils, pens, colored pencils
Construction paper, glue, small pieces of paper

How to Do It

1. Cover your shoebox with construction paper. Decorate as you desire.
2. Cut a slit (like a penny bank) on the top of the cover.
3. Place the goodness box in the kitchen. Set the slips of paper and a pencil next to it.
4. Tell your family how to use it. Every time they see someone doing good deeds for others, they should write it down on a slip of paper. For example, "I saw Stephanie help clean Melanie's room." At the end of the week, gather your family together and read the slips of paper.

11

WEEK ELEVEN SUNDAY ____________
(DATE)

Theme for the Week: Humility

Key Verse for the Week

Be completely humble and gentle; be patient, bearing with one another in love.

—Ephesians 4:2

Bible Reading: Ephesians 4:1-2

Blue Ribbons, Green Ribbons

During a school awards ceremony, I watched two girls show very different attitudes when they received their blue, first-place ribbons. One girl took her ribbon and strutted back to her seat. The other girl accepted her ribbon, thanked the coach, and quietly slipped back into her seat. The first girl showed pride; the second girl showed humility.

Out of the sixty students who were competing for ribbons, I wanted to award a gold trophy to the girl who was holding only one ribbon. It was a green participation ribbon, one that each student received. When the ceremony was finished, she didn't dash out of the room in tears. Instead, she congratulated the other girls for earning so many ribbons.

Being humble—whether you're holding eight blue ribbons or one green participation ribbon—is rarely easy. Humility, our theme for the week, is the opposite of pride. It's saying thank you and modestly accepting your blue ribbons. It's refraining from saying "That's not fair" when all you get is one green ribbon.

Humility is God's will for our lives: "Be completely humble and gentle; be patient, bearing with one another in love" (Ephesians 4:2).

Something to Think About

Winning blue (or green) ribbons is not a problem. What's important is your attitude when you accept them. Will you show pride or humility?

Dear Jesus,

I praise you for ______________________________

____

____

I'm sorry for ______________________________

____

____

I ask you for ______________________________

____

____

I thank you for ______________________________

____

______________________________ Amen.

S	K	R	D	D	M	S	S	E	N	E	L	B	M	U	H
A	S	Y	Z	D	R	R	L	W	G	D	J	H	T	J	T
R	L	E	T	A	L	K	I	M	X	C	Z	X	F	I	B
R	O	G	N	S	Z	J	A	X	I	H	I	T	E	K	K
O	W	G	T	E	E	R	K	H	T	W	M	C	N	Z	V
G	L	Q	L	A	L	D	H	D	U	D	N	S	N	B	Y
A	I	A	Y	P	P	T	O	B	W	O	S	A	C	E	H
N	N	O	K	T	Y	Q	N	M	C	E	S	U	O	F	F
C	E	X	B	E	Q	X	X	E	N	A	T	P	Q	P	S
E	S	Y	N	E	U	M	V	I	G	P	V	H	J	T	S
V	S	E	B	P	G	A	T	E	U	S	R	C	F	Y	E
Z	K	T	E	U	N	H	U	P	G	F	X	I	L	K	N
Y	E	J	E	I	G	F	H	T	T	L	T	X	D	J	K
N	H	A	T	U	B	E	S	R	G	C	I	C	Q	E	E
Q	D	Y	A	M	M	C	G	O	R	A	C	Z	M	L	E
G	L	H	P	L	K	B	I	X	U	M	T	P	R	R	M

Humility Word Search

Find the words that define humility:

GENTLENESS
HUMBLENESS
LOWLINESS
MEEKNESS
MODESTY

Find the words that are the opposite of humility:

ARROGANCE
CONCEIT
HAUGHTINESS
PRIDE
VANITY

Theme for the Week: Humility

Key Verse for the Week

Be completely humble and gentle; be patient, bearing with one another in love.

—Ephesians 4:2

Bible Reading: 1 Peter 5:5-6

What Are You Wearing?

Note: Look in the mirror for two minutes before you begin reading this devotional.

What are you wearing right now? Are you wearing a smile that can brighten up your classroom at school? Do you only wear your smile when you're looking at the cool kids? Or does it radiate just as brightly when you're with the not-so-popular, hard-to-love students?

What are you wearing right now? Are your ears ready to listen to the problems and joys of others? Or might you just as well be wearing ear plugs because you'd much rather talk about yourself than waste time listening to other people tell their stories?

What are you wearing right now? Are you wearing eyes that are constantly looking for ways to build others up? Or are you watching for opportunities to tell others about the great things you've been doing?

What are you wearing right now? Are you wearing humility? "All of you, clothe yourselves with humility toward one another, because, 'God opposes the proud but gives grace to the humble'" (1 Peter 5:5b). Dress your best for God today—clothe yourself in humility!

Something to Think About

Write 1 Peter 5:5b on a notecard. Post it in the middle of the mirror that you use to get ready each morning. Let it remind you to clothe yourself in humility as you prepare for a new day!

Dear Jesus,

I praise you for ______________________________

____

____

I'm sorry for ______________________________

____

____

I ask you for ______________________________

____

____

I thank you for ______________________________

____

______________________________ Amen.

Dressing My Best

How many times have you yelled from your bedroom, "I don't have anything to wear!"? Today's project will help you get your clothes organized and make your parents happy too!

What You Need

2 cardboard boxes, markers

How to Do It

1. Mark one cardboard box "too small."
2. Mark the second box "never wear."
3. Clean out your dresser drawers, one at a time, sorting out the ones for the boxes.
4. Neatly fold the remaining clothes and put them back in your drawers.
5. Ask your parents to help you deliver the clothes in the boxes to an organization like Goodwill or a local mission store.
6. Remember that no matter how many clothes you own, God is most concerned that you clothe yourself with humility.

Theme for the Week: Humility

Key Verse for the Week

Be completely humble and gentle; be patient, bearing with one another in love.

—Ephesians 4:2

Bible Reading: Luke 14:7-11

Eating Humble Pie

You might be eating humble pie if you . . .

- brag before a race that you're the fastest runner in the class and then come in fifth place.
- tell everyone that your family is flying to Europe for summer vacation and then your trip actually ends up to be a picnic at a local park.
- let everyone know what a fabulous history report you wrote and then get a C+ on it.

Jesus tells a parable about humility in Luke 14:7-11. He talks about wedding guests who are taking their places at the dinner table. It's better to sit in a lower place and have the host move you to a place of honor, says Jesus, than it is to take a place of honor and be humiliated when the host sends you to a lower place. "For everyone who exalts himself will be humbled, and he who humbles himself will be exalted" (Luke 14:11).

I don't know how many wedding feasts you'll be invited to this year, but one thing I am sure of: This parable (a story with a heavenly meaning) still holds true for you and me today. Wherever you go—weddings, school, picnics, or church—keep pride out of your words and actions, and wear an attitude of humility.

Something to Think About

When's the last time you had to eat humble pie?

Dear Jesus,

I praise you for ______________________________

____

____

I'm sorry for ______________________________

____

____

I ask you for ______________________________

____

____

I thank you for ______________________________

____

______________________________ Amen.

Mud Pie

What You Need

Store-bought cookie-crumb pie shell
6 cups (1.44 L) chocolate ice cream, softened
1 cup (.24 L) fudge topping
¾ cup (.18 L) crushed chocolate cookies
4 cups (.96 L) whipped topping

How to Do It

1. Ask an adult for permission to work in the kitchen.
2. Fill the pie shell with half of the chocolate ice cream.
3. Freeze for 30 minutes.
4. Spread the fudge topping over the ice cream. Freeze for 15 minutes.
5. Top with remaining ice cream, whipped topping, and crushed cookies.
6. Freeze for at least 3 hours.
7. When you're sharing your mud pie with guests, talk about eating humble pie!

Theme for the Week: Humility

Key Verse for the Week

Be completely humble and gentle; be patient, bearing with one another in love.

—Ephesians 4:2

Bible Reading: Philippians 2:5-11

Imitating Christ

When it comes to humility, Philippians 2:5 lays it on the line: "Your attitude should be the same as that of Christ." Did you catch that? It doesn't say, "It would be nice if your attitude would be . . . " or, "If you feel like it, your attitude could be . . . " It says, "Your attitude should be the same as that of Christ."

Christians need to imitate Jesus. He showed his disciples a self-sacrificing attitude of humility and love for other people.

Today's Bible passage has lots of examples of Christ's humility:

- "[He] did not consider equality with God something to be grasped" (verse 6).
- "[He] made himself nothing, taking the very nature of a servant" (verse 7).
- "He humbled himself and became obedient to death" (verse 8).

It's hard for this world to comprehend Christ's attitude of humility and love for others. It doesn't make sense that the King of kings and Lord of lords would leave the glories of heaven to be born in a barn (Luke 2:6-7) or to wash dirty feet (John 13:1-17). Remember that everything Jesus did was done because he loves us so much. We can show our love to Jesus by imitating his humility.

Something to Think About

Is your attitude self-sacrificing or self-promoting? Ask God to help you develop a Christ-like attitude of humility.

Dear Jesus,

I praise you for ______________________________

____

____

I'm sorry for ______________________________

____

____

I ask you for ______________________________

____

____

I thank you for ______________________________

____

______________________________ Amen.

A Humble Little Word Puzzle

Change each of the numbers into letters and discover a Bible verse that teaches God's children about humility.

A	B	C	D	E	F	G	H	I	J	K	L	M	N	O	P	Q	R	S	T	U	V	W	X	Y	Z
1	2	3	4	5	6	7	8	9	10	11	12	13	14	15	16	17	18	19	20	21	22	23	24	25	26

__ __   __ __ __ __ __ __ __ __   __ __ __ __ __ __ __ __   __ __ __ __ __ __

9 14   8 21 13 9 12 9 20 25   3 15 14 19 9 4 5 18   15 20 8 5 18 19

__ __ __ __ __ __   __ __ __ __   __ __ __ __ __ __ __ __ __ __.

2 5 20 20 5 18   20 8 1 14   25 15 21 18 19 5 12 22 5 19

Answer: Philippians 2:3b

Theme for the Week: Humility

Key Verse for the Week

Be completely humble and gentle; be patient, bearing with one another in love.

—Ephesians 4:2

Bible Reading: Isaiah 66:2

Honoring Humility

Who does the world applaud and cheer?

___ The star athlete who scores the winning basket in a basketball game.

___ The man down the street who delivers food to the homeless.

Who does the world applaud and cheer?

___ The model on the cover of a teen magazine.

___ The teenage girl who tutors elementary students in math.

The world honors star athletes, models, and movie stars. God honors those who humbly go about Jesus' business serving others. "This is the one I esteem: he who is humble and contrite in spirit, and trembles at my word" (Isaiah 66:2).

God esteems those who have contrite or humble attitudes and actions—those who put others before themselves. God wants us to "tremble at his word" by studying the Bible and praying to God each day.

Who is cheering for you? Does the world applaud you because of your athletic ability or good looks? Or is God cheering for you because you're always trying to serve Jesus with a humble and contrite spirit?

Something to Think About

When you honor others with your applause and cheers, what standard do you use?

___ the world's standard

___ God's standard

Dear Jesus,

I praise you for ________________________________

____

____

I'm sorry for ________________________________

____

____

I ask you for ________________________________

____

____

I thank you for ________________________________

____

________________________________ Amen.

Treasure Box

Personalize a treasure box for yourself as a reminder to treasure God's standards, not the world's standards.

What You Need

Acrylic paints or paint pens

Plastic box that has small compartments (you can find these in the craft, hobby, or fishing departments of discount stores).

How to Do It

1. Use your acrylic paints or paint pens to decorate the top and sides of the box. Write your name and draw your favorite designs.
2. Store your "mini" treasures in the small compartments. It works well for beads, candy, coins, or jewelry.

Theme for the Week: Humility

Key Verse for the Week

Be completely humble and gentle; be patient, bearing with one another in love.

—Ephesians 4:2

Bible Reading: Titus 3:1-2

Showing Humility

The Bible says we are to "show true humility toward all men" (Titus 3:2). You can follow Christ's example and show true humility to all people through your words and actions.

With your words . . .
When you ask people about themselves instead of only talking about yourself, you are showing true humility. When you encourage and build other people up instead of talking about how great you are, you are showing true humility. Each time you replace "me and myself" with "you and yourself," you are imitating Christ's true humility.

With your actions . . .
When you try your best to please God instead of trying to earn the praise and applause of others, you're showing true humility. When you win awards and give God the glory and thanks, you're demonstrating true humility. You're imitating Christ's humility when you have a servant's heart that quietly does God's will instead of boastfully making sure everyone knows that you're doing good things.

Show true humility to the people around you, and you will be a living testimony to the great and awesome God you serve!

Something to Think About

Humility is not like show-and-tell. It's more like hide-and-seek. (Hide your good works from people and seek to give God the glory.)

Dear Jesus,

I praise you for ______________________________

____

____

I'm sorry for ______________________________

____

____

I ask you for ______________________________

____

____

I thank you for ______________________________

____

______________________________ Amen.

Hide-and-Seek

Round up your little brothers, sisters, cousins, and neighbor kids for a game of hide-and-seek!

What You Need

A small object (coin, button, or paper clip)

How to Do It

1. Decide where your boundaries are going to be. In one or two rooms of the house? In the backyard? Have everyone agree.
2. Everyone should close their eyes or go to a different room while one person hides the small object.
3. The first person in the group to find the object gets to hide it the next time.
4. This game can entertain kids of all ages. (I've even seen grandpas and grandmas really enjoy this activity!)

WEEK ELEVEN — SATURDAY ____________ (DATE)

Theme for the Week: Humility

Key Verse for the Week

Write the key verse for the week on the lines below.

____

____

____

—Ephesians 4:2

This Week I Learned . . .

Sunday
I need to be humble in whatever situation I'm in—whether I'm holding a first-place blue ribbon or a green participation ribbon. (Ephesians 4:1-2)

Monday
Each morning I should check what I'm wearing. I need to make sure my smile, my ears, and my eyes are all clothed in humility. (1 Peter 5:5-6)

Tuesday
When I follow Jesus' teaching about humility in the parable about the wedding feast, I can avoid eating humble pie. (Luke 14:7-11)

Wednesday
My attitude towards humility should be the same as that of Christ. (Philippians 2:5-11)

Thursday
The world praises movie stars, great athletes, and beautiful people. God honors those who have a humble and contrite spirit. (Isaiah 66:2)

Friday
I can show humility towards all people through the words I speak and the things I do. (Titus 3:1-2)

Something to Think About

How can you imitate Christ's humility for the people around you?

____

____

____

Dear Jesus,

I praise you for ______________________________

____

____

I'm sorry for ______________________________

____

____

I ask you for ______________________________

____

____

I thank you for ______________________________

____

______________________________ Amen.

Fruit Kabobs

What You Need

Fruit—pineapple (fresh or canned), apples, kiwis, bananas, strawberries, assorted melons

Kabob skewers

How to Do It

1. Cut the fruit into bite-size pieces. Use plastic knives, cookie cutters, and melon scoops to cut your fruit into different shapes. Be creative!
2. To make one kabob, carefully push fruits onto the kabob skewer. Alternate different colors and shapes for a colorful, tasty treat.
3. Make as many as you wish. (Make sure you have enough people to eat them all!)

WEEK TWELVE — SUNDAY ________ (DATE)

Theme for the Week: Perseverance

Key Verse for the Week

Therefore, since we are surrounded by such a great cloud of witnesses, let us throw off everything that hinders and the sin that so easily entangles, and let us run with perseverance the race marked out for us.

—Hebrews 12:1

Bible Reading: Hebrews 12:1-2

Perseverance Running

When I was in the ninth grade, I was a member of our school's track team. Each member of the team found her specialty. Mine was the mile run. After ten weeks of track, I gained strong leg muscles, earned fancy medals, and—most importantly—learned perseverance.

After four laps around the track, there were times when my legs grew tired and I wanted to quit, but then I would hear my coach and teammates cheering for me and renewing my strength. When I wanted to give up, I'd focus on the finish line and the possibility of earning a medal.

Christians are also involved in a race that requires perseverance. "Therefore, since we are surrounded by such a great cloud of witnesses, let us throw off everything that hinders and the sin that so easily entangles, and let us run with perseverance the race marked out for us" (Hebrews 12:1).

The Christian life is like a long-distance race. Sometimes sin and Satan will make you want to quit—but remember that Jesus is cheering you on and giving you strength. When you want to give up, focus on the finish line—eternal life with Jesus Christ in heaven.

Something to Think About

The Christian life is not a short sprint. It requires perseverance!

Dear Jesus,

I praise you for ______________________________

____

____

I'm sorry for ______________________________

____

____

I ask you for ______________________________

____

____

I thank you for ______________________________

____

______________________________ Amen.

Persevering Plants

This project will take two or three days, but the end result is worth the wait!

What You Need

Fine-tipped felt markers
1 empty eggshell with top ¼ broken off
1 small napkin ring
3 damp cotton balls
⅛ teaspoon alfalfa seeds

How to Do It

1. Set the empty eggshell on the napkin ring.
2. Draw a face on the eggshell with the markers.
3. Place damp cotton balls inside eggshell.
4. Sprinkle alfalfa seeds over the cotton. Keep the cotton damp.
5. Place the eggshell in a sunny window. In a few days the seeds will begin to sprout.
6. When the egg's "hair" (alfalfa sprouts) begins to grow, you'll have to give your eggshell a "haircut." Persevere and have fun!

12

W E E K T W E L V E M O N D A Y ____________
(DATE)

Theme for the Week: Perseverance

Key Verse for the Week

Therefore, since we are surrounded by such a great cloud of witnesses, let us throw off everything that hinders and the sin that so easily entangles, and let us run with perseverance the race marked out for us.

—*Hebrews 12:1*

Bible Reading: 2 Peter 1:5-9

Productive Perseverance

Second Peter 1:5-9 lists eight fruits that need to grow in a Christian's life. Write the fruits below. (The first letter of each fruit is listed for you!)

F________________ S________________

B________________ G________________

P________________ L________________

K________________ G________________

Each fall the two apple trees in my yard bend toward the ground because of the heavy weight of all the apples that are hanging on their branches. There are always too many apples for our family to eat!

God wants us to be like my apple trees! We need to persevere in our faith and grow the fruits of the Spirit in our lives. The fruits that you listed should be growing abundantly in your life, just like the apples are growing abundantly on my trees!

The Bible says, "For if you possess these qualities [fruits] in increasing measure, they will keep you from being ineffective and unproductive in your knowledge of our Lord Jesus Christ" (2 Peter 1:8). You will grow the fruits of the Spirit when you persevere in your faith and continue to learn more and more about Jesus.

Something to Think About

Which one of the fruits you listed is most abundant in your life? Write it down in this space: ______________________________

Dear Jesus,

I praise you for ______________________________

____

____

I'm sorry for ______________________________

____

____

I ask you for ______________________________

____

____

I thank you for ______________________________

____

______________________________ Amen.

Obstacle Course

The next time neighbor kids or cousins are at your home, create an obstacle course. It's double perseverance—first, you'll have to persevere in setting it up. Second, you'll have to persevere while you run through it!

What You Need

Jump ropes, hula hoops, balls, Frisbees . . . (You're limited only by your imagination!)

How to Do It

Here are some activities you may include in your obstacle course:

- Jump rope 25 times
- Hang a hula hoop from a tree and throw a ball or Frisbee through it
- Skip, hop, or dance
- Do three backwards somersaults
- Count to 50

W E E K T W E L V E T U E S D A Y ________ (DATE)

Theme for the Week: Perseverance

Key Verse for the Week

Therefore, since we are surrounded by such a great cloud of witnesses, let us throw off everything that hinders and the sin that so easily entangles, and let us run with perseverance the race marked out for us.

—Hebrews 12:1

Bible Reading: James 1:12

Perseverance Under Trial

Perseverance is . . .

- delivering 30 newspapers in 30 minutes.

Perseverance under trial is . . .

- delivering 30 newspapers in 30 minutes *in the rain!*

Perseverance is . . .

- learning how to play the violin.

Perseverance under trial is . . .

- learning how to play the violin when *two of your fingers are broken!*

Perseverance is . . .

- witnessing for Jesus every day.

Perseverance under trial is . . .

- witnessing for Jesus every day when *your classmates make fun of you because you're a Christian!*

James 1:12 says, "Blessed is the man who perseveres under trial, because when he has stood the test, he will receive the crown of life that God has promised to those who love him." When your faith perseveres under trial, you will receive the crown of life—eternity with Jesus Christ!

Something to Think About

Thinking about the glories of heaven can make trials seem trivial!

Dear Jesus,

I praise you for ______________________________

____

____

I'm sorry for ______________________________

____

____

I ask you for ______________________________

____

____

I thank you for ______________________________

____

______________________________ Amen.

Perseverance Pops

What You Need

1 cup (.24 L) seedless watermelon chunks
1 cup (.24 L) orange juice
1 cup (.24 L) water
Paper cups
Plastic spoons

How to Do It

1. Blend watermelon, orange juice, and water in a blender.
2. Pour mixture into paper cups.
3. Place in freezer.
4. When the pops are partially frozen, insert the spoons for handles.
5. When your Perseverance Pops are completely frozen, pour hot water over the bottoms of the cups to remove them easily.
6. Share these tasty treats with your family or friends, and tell them what you've been learning this week about perseverance.

Theme for the Week: Perseverance

Key Verse for the Week

Therefore, since we are surrounded by such a great cloud of witnesses, let us throw off everything that hinders and the sin that so easily entangles, and let us run with perseverance the race marked out for us.

—Hebrews 12:1

Bible Reading: Luke 8:4-15

Persevering Seed

Jesus tells a parable about what happens to seed that is planted in four types of soil.

Path: The seed that fell on the path died because it was trampled on. This seed represents people who hear the Bible but don't believe because Satan "tramples" their faith.

Rock: The seed that fell on the rock died because it was too dry to grow. This seed represents people who hear the Bible but don't believe because they're not growing through prayer and Bible study.

Weedy field: This seed died because it couldn't grow in all the weeds. It represents people who hear the Bible but don't believe because their faith dies when trouble comes.

Good soil: The seed that fell in the good soil grew. This seed represents people who hear the Bible and believe. They persevere and grow in their faith.

Jesus said, "But the seed on good soil stands for those with a noble and good heart, who hear the word, retain it, and by persevering produce a crop" (Luke 8:15). Christians must read and study the Bible (good soil) and grow in their faith. Be a persevering seed!

Something to Think About

What kind of "ground" is your faith growing on? Circle one.

Path Rock Weedy field Good Soil

Dear Jesus,

I praise you for ______________________________

____

____

I'm sorry for ______________________________

____

____

I ask you for ______________________________

____

____

I thank you for ______________________________

____

______________________________ Amen.

Perseverance Chain

Think of a goal—something you'd like to accomplish during the next month. Here are a few examples:

- Shoot (and make) 30 layups or baskets a day.
- Read _____ (fill in the number) books in a month.
- Make your bed every morning without being reminded.

Make this chain to help you keep track of your goal!

What You Need

Construction paper, scissors, glue

How to Do It

1. Cut the construction paper lengthwise for each link of the chain.
2. Each day after you've completed your project, write the date and what you did on the link of the chain. (For example, June 6—Finished reading *Charlotte's Web*. Or June 6—Made my bed without Mom reminding me.)
3. Glue the links together. Watch your chain grow during the next month!

Theme for the Week: Perseverance

Key Verse for the Week

Therefore, since we are surrounded by such a great cloud of witnesses, let us throw off everything that hinders and the sin that so easily entangles, and let us run with perseverance the race marked out for us.

—Hebrews 12:1

Bible Reading: 2 Thessalonians 3:4-5

Christ's Perseverance

Have you ever worked on a difficult project like a really long book report that had to be typed, or a complicated science project that took lots of hard work to finish? If so, you'll be able to identify with the train engine in the book *The Little Engine That Could.* Pulling a long line of cars up a steep hill looked like an overwhelming job to that little engine. He didn't quit, though! He went chugging right up the hill by saying, "I think I can . . . I think I can . . . I think I can . . ."

That's a fun, encouraging story to remember for things like school projects and messy rooms. But when it comes to the things that really matter in your life—things like praying and reading your Bible every day, loving your enemies, forgiving your family members, and putting other people's needs before your own wants—you need Christ's perseverance.

"May the Lord direct your hearts into God's love and Christ's perseverance" (2 Thessalonians 3:5). Jesus Christ lived in this sinful world and never, ever—not even one time—gave up on sinners. When you want to give up on things that are important in your life, imitate Christ's perseverance.

Something to Think About

Read *The Little Engine That Could* for a fun story. Read the Bible for lessons about persevering in your faith.

Dear Jesus,

I praise you for ______________________________

____

____

I'm sorry for ______________________________

____

____

I ask you for ______________________________

____

____

I thank you for ______________________________

____

______________________________ Amen.

How Long?

When it comes to working on a big project, Noah has to be one of the finalists for a perseverance prize. Read Genesis 6:14-16 to discover God's instructions on how to build an ark. Measure it out for yourself and get an idea of how much perseverance that project took!

What You Need

A fairly quiet, large parking lot or long sidewalk
25-foot tape measure
Chalk

How to Do It

1. Have someone help you measure the lengths with the tape measure.
2. With your piece of chalk, make a mark every 10 feet.
3. Measure the following ark dimensions: 450 feet long; 75 feet wide; 45 feet high.

Theme for the Week: Perseverance

Key Verse for the Week

Therefore, since we are surrounded by such a great cloud of witnesses, let us throw off everything that hinders and the sin that so easily entangles, and let us run with perseverance the race marked out for us.

—Hebrews 12:1

Bible Reading: Hebrews 10:36-37

The Perseverance Prize

"And the winner is . . ." If you've ever watched an awards program or game show on TV, you've heard those words. Winners receive trophies, money, flowers, and trips . . . all kinds of goodies.

The winners must be excited to get their gifts. But eventually the trophies will gather dust, the money will be spent, the flowers will die, and the trips will be just a memory. Those gifts—like all material possessions—just don't last.

Today's Bible reading talks about a prize that will be given to Christians who persevere in their faith. It's a prize that's given to those who believe in Jesus and never quit trying to obey him. This prize will last forever. It'll never rust, disappear, or die.

Hebrews 10:36 says, "You need to persevere so that when you have done the will of God, you will receive what he has promised." What is the prize that you are promised? "He [Jesus] who is coming will come and will not delay" (verse 37). Jesus is coming to take you to heaven to be with him forever and ever. No earthly prize can compare with eternity in heaven. I can't wait! How about you?

Something to Think About

If you love Jesus, write your name in the blank.

And the winner of an eternity in heaven with Jesus, her Lord, is ________________!

Dear Jesus,

I praise you for ______________________________

____

____

I'm sorry for ______________________________

____

____

I ask you for ______________________________

____

____

I thank you for ______________________________

____

______________________________ Amen.

Pudding Sandwiches

Make these for tonight's dessert or a bedtime snack. Tell your family what you learned about perseverance this week and the promised prize—eternity with Jesus!

What You Need

1½ cups (.36 L) cold milk
1 package instant chocolate pudding mix
¼ to ½ cup (.6-.12 L) peanut butter
15 whole graham crackers

How to Do It

1. In a mixing bowl, combine the milk, pudding mix, and peanut butter.
2. Beat on low speed for 2 minutes. Let the mixture stand for 5 minutes.
3. Break the whole graham crackers in half.
4. Spread pudding mixture over half of the crackers. Top the sandwiches with the remaining crackers.
5. Wrap pudding sandwiches and freeze until firm.

Theme for the Week: Perseverance

Key Verse for the Week

Write the key verse for the week on the lines below.

____

____

____

—Hebrews 12:1

This Week I Learned . . .

Sunday
As a Christian, my life is like a long-distance race. Jesus is cheering for me and giving me strength to persevere in my faith. (Hebrews 12:1-2)

Monday
When I persevere in my faith, the fruit of the Spirit will grow abundantly in my life. (2 Peter 1:5-9)

Tuesday
There are times that it's difficult to be a Christian. I will be blessed with eternity in heaven when I persevere under trial. (James 1:12)

Wednesday
My faith needs to grow on good soil. When I read and study the Bible and persevere in my faith, I will grow as a Christian! (Luke 8:4-15)

Thursday
Christ never, ever—not even one time—gives up on sinners, including me! I need to follow Jesus' example of perfect perseverance. (2 Thessalonians 3:4-5)

Friday
If I persevere in my faith, I will receive the prize of eternity in heaven with Jesus, my Lord. Come quickly, Lord Jesus! (Hebrews 10:36-37)

Something to Think About

What did you learn about perseverance this week?

____

____

____

Dear Jesus,

I praise you for ____

____

____

I'm sorry for ____

____

____

I ask you for ____

____

____

I thank you for ____

____

____ Amen.

Word Puzzle

P is for perseverance, the theme for the week. Beginning with the first P in the puzzle, cross out every other letter. (Every letter you cross out should be a P.) Discover the best way to run with perseverance.

PLPEPTPUPSPRPUPNPWPIPTPHPPPEPRPSPEPVPEPRPAPNPCPEPTPHPEPRPAPCPEPMPAPRPKPEPDPO

PUPTPFPOPRPUPSPLPEPTPUPSPFPIPXPOPUPRPEPYPEPSPOPNPJPEPSPUPSPTPHPEPAPUPTPHPOPR

PAPNPDPPPEPRPFPEPCPTPEPRPOPFPOPUPRPFPAPIPTPHP!

To check your answer, see Hebrews 12:1b-2a

For your privacy we have given you a cover that closes. Simply fold the back cover over the front, and insert the tab into the slot on the front cover.